PRAISE FOR BOB

I met Bob McCall at a safety seminar he was presenting at in Chicago, and immediately the president of our company and I knew we had to bring him in to help transform our thinking on leadership. We had recently combined two companies that used to be together over twenty-five years prior, and although they were only two miles apart, the cultures were very different. After Bob's training it started a new excitement about leadership and how it can change lives, regardless of your location.

This became the catalyst for creating our Kruger Brown Companies' way of leadership. Soon we had a list of expectations, as well as what associates can expect from the company, and everyone was holding each other to a higher level. Everyone understood what we could expect from each other. Just as Bob taught us, our preshift meetings were suddenly engaging and filled with value and allowed others to step up as leaders.

The excitement that Bob brings with his training engages everyone in the room and does not allow anyone to hide. His passion for leadership overflows in his interactions with everyone he meets. The uplifting style that Bob uses to coach others has changed our environment to be more positive and uplifting.

We have put one-third of our six hundred associates through this training, with more to come. We cannot thank Bob enough for lighting the flame on leadership and inspiring our associates so that this new culture can live on for years to come, creating a legacy of how Kruger Brown leaders lead.

—Todd Spencer

Vice president of human resources, Kruger Brown Companies

I had the pleasure of listening and meeting Bob back in the fall of 2017 while attending a conference in Charlotte, North Carolina. I was immediately blown away by his experience, industry knowledge, strong business acumen, and most importantly his passion for leadership and personal growth. His vibrant personality and his ability to create a personal connection with every member of the audience was not only impressive but also inspiring. Without any hesitation, I told my colleague sitting next to me that Bob needed to be a part of our annual safety and risk conference. Since then, Bob has trained and inspired every level of our organization to awaken the leader within us, and to continue to be a leader and the company of choice in our industry.

—Giovanny J. Morales

EHS manager, S. T. Wooten Corporation

Leadership training begins with a room that's on fire! Bob McCall is the spark that created the combustion within our organization. We know of no one else who can command and connect with a room of three hundred highway construction workers, from CEO to laborer, giving an inspired leadership message that everyone can apply back at the jobsite. And he did it time and again, with no loss of attention or enthusiasm, until each of our one thousand employees were all touched by a message that now guides us and allows leaders to build and maintain high-performing teams.

Bob's positive effect and message is consistently echoed in our employees' feedback. Our leaders cite his ability to connect, inspire, and thoughtfully challenge them. And they rise to Bob's challenge, like a longtime foreman who inspires his team and provokes a positive mindset with daily toolbox talks that begin with, "This is the year of change." You, too, can light up your "year of change" and fully discover your leadership potential with Bob McCall and his inspirational, challenging message contained in this book.

—Mandy Kerr

Learning and development coordinator, S. T. Wooten

Bob brings a contagious energy and enthusiasm and a different way to approach leadership, with an emphasis on engagement and building trust with the team. He makes it clear that high-functioning teams start with a leader who continuously encourages and reinforces success with positive team interactions. Bob believes that one way to succeed is to give it everything, and he reinforces this message with his own commitment to our company and his message of team growth and support.

—Caroline Feldhausen

Utility professional

AWAKEN
THE LEADER IN YOU

AWAKEN
THE LEADER IN YOU

HOW TO BUILD A **HIGH-PERFORMANCE TEAM**

BOB McCALL

Published by Advantage, Charleston, South Carolina.
Member of Advantage Media Group.

ADVANTAGE is a registered trademark, and the Advantage colophon is a trademark of Advantage Media Group, Inc.

Printed in the United States of America.

10 9 8 7 6 5 4 3 2 1

ISBN: 978-1-64225-114-2
LCCN: 2019918871

Cover and layout design by George Stevens.

This publication is designed to provide accurate and authoritative information in regard to the subject matter covered. It is sold with the understanding that the publisher is not engaged in rendering legal, accounting, or other professional services. If legal advice or other expert assistance is required, the services of a competent professional person should be sought.

 Advantage Media Group is proud to be a part of the Tree Neutral® program. Tree Neutral offsets the number of trees consumed in the production and printing of this book by taking proactive steps such as planting trees in direct proportion to the number of trees used to print books. To learn more about Tree Neutral, please visit **www.treeneutral.com**.

Advantage Media Group is a publisher of business, self-improvement, and professional development books and online learning. We help entrepreneurs, business leaders, and professionals share their Stories, Passion, and Knowledge to help others Learn & Grow. Do you have a manuscript or book idea that you would like us to consider for publishing? Please visit **advantagefamily.com** or call **1.866.775.1696**.

I would like to dedicate this book to my parents, who believed I could do great things. Their willingness to sacrifice to send my sister and me to private schools to ensure that we had a great education and then continue to help us get through college made all the difference. Their support and belief inspired me to be my best in all that I do.

CONTENTS

ACKNOWLEDGMENTS

Thanks to Mike McDevitt for his help in making this book come to life.

I would like to thank God for the insight and ability to write this book.

FOREWORD

Rachel White, MBA, CUSP

A few years ago, I had the privilege of hearing Bob McCall speak at an IP conference in Kentucky. He presented at the opening ceremony, and I was so inspired by the end of the talk. He spoke of being engaged, caring about people, doing the right things. At the time, I was a field safety coordinator. His talk gave me a vision for how I wanted to behave if I ever assumed a leadership position at my company.

A few years later, Bob presented again at another IP conference. He taught a session called "Building a High-Performance Team." At the time I was supervising a group of seventeen men—mechanical substation journeymen and substation testing technicians. I left that conference inspired. I also left the conference with some language, best practices, and leadership principles that I immediately incorporated into my work group.

The message that Bob had was important! As I implemented the principles into my work group, people began to notice a difference. My manager, his manager, and the executive directors began to compliment my work group on a noticeable change in attitude; we were less negative and more team oriented. They helped me come to conclusions. They helped me replace equipment, and they helped me improve the overall morale of the work group.

One of my coworkers also attended Bob's training. We began

talking to our safety and training group about getting Bob to come to our company. We wanted our entire company to hear Bob's message. In 2019 we made that desire a reality. Our company hired Bob for a complete week. Our schedule included Bob appearing at over ten sites, and then we live broadcasted him to additional sites.

While Bob presented to our company, I had the privilege of being his chaperone. The information that I learned from Bob during the week of his safety tour was life changing. He talked to me about specific things I could do to help move my career forward. We talked about mentorship, résumé building, interview preparation, questions I needed to ask during interviews, and being the right fit for a position. I listened. I put all the tools into practice as I began working toward the next step in my career.

I am so thankful that I had the opportunity to meet Bob. I learned about leadership principles and personal development. Within six months I obtained a position in my company as the senior manager of distribution system operations. I am implementing all the principles that I learned from Bob, and I am setting expectations for my team members and their team members so we can build a high-performing team and create an environment for top potential performers.

WHAT DOES IT TAKE TO GET THE BEST OUT OF PEOPLE?

What would it take to inspire your team, your staff, and your colleagues to be their best? To help them reach heights greater than they'd ever imagined? No matter what business you're in or how many people work under your management, the answer can be summed up in one word: *leadership*. Great leaders know how to motivate, encourage, and help others to perform at their highest levels. Having said that, there is a hard reality that I must mention. When you start a journey of excellence, not everyone will make it—not because they don't have what it takes to get there, but because they're not willing to do what it takes. Leaders must know that you *can't change everyone*; team members must be willing to go on the journey. So what does it take to be the leader whom team members are eager to follow and will strive to please?

My mom used to tell us kids that if we *know* better, we're expected to *do* better—and by the time you've finished reading this book, you *will* know better. I'm going to give you the blueprint, the insights, and the confidence to step forward and become the best leader you can be, because that's where it all starts—not by remaking your team, but by making a better *you*. That better you will inspire the best in others. Here's a statement I want you to get very familiar with, and I will repeat it many times throughout the book: "A leader's attitude is contagious." The leader is responsible for the way the team feels and acts and for the culture in which they work. With this knowledge, a leader can no longer walk around thinking they can act any old way.

Follow along with this very possible situation: if a leader simply coasts along and stops growing their leadership skills, thinking, "I got this," or projects the attitude that they have been there a significant number of years and can rest on their laurels and coast to retirement, the team will sense it. The team will sense the coasting attitude in the leader's conversation, tone of voice, and body language, and the team will decide to emulate the leader and coast or slow down as well. Leaders keep their team from growing when they stop growing in their leadership skills. Likewise, leaders motivate teams when they themselves are motivated.

As a recognized authority on leadership, John Maxwell said, "Everything rises and falls on leadership"—and he was 100 percent right. If you refuse to settle for second best in yourself and strive to improve your leadership skills, your team also will see that and will grow along with you. If you're willing to transform your leadership style and adopt the leadership attributes I'll lay out for you in these pages, you'll have the tools you need to create an environment in which people can perform at their highest levels, and be eager to do so.

Make this year your year of action, and by that, I mean the year in which you commit to transforming your leadership into a force that connects your team to each other and to you. Commit to deepening your understanding of what moves and motivates your team. Commit to creating the environment in which they can do their best, but most importantly, it all starts with you!

CHAPTER ONE

OUT OF THE GATE

You don't become a champion just because you win a game. A champion
is someone you become through a process of self-improvement,
sacrifices, service, and, yes, the attainment of goals that are normally
out of reach of all except those willing to pay the price.

—Lee Labrada

I n 1982 I was hired as a field engineer for the Bechtel Power
Company to work at the Belle River power plant in Saint Clair,
Michigan. I was just twenty-three, and suddenly I was a field
engineer with experienced, older union craftspeople on my
team. How could I motivate this experienced team, most of whom
were about twice my age? How could I get the best out of them?
How could I gain their respect? I wasn't sure, but I knew I needed to
understand leadership better than I did if we were going to succeed.
Fortunately, I'd had some good examples of what leadership looks
like growing up, and I reflected on them as I considered what that
meant.

My Little League coach, Coach Delaney, was someone whose
commitment to being a good leader made an impact on me at an

early age. Because my dad worked night shifts, he wasn't around during the day to help me build my baseball skills, so Coach Delaney stepped in, spending his personal time after practice to help me be a better hitter. The day I hit a home run in our Little League championship game, I felt pretty good about myself, yet when I stopped to consider it, I saw that the run was really a gift to me from my coach. The realization that I owed my success to him in some ways helped me realize that a good leader is willing to go above and beyond to help those he leads to grow.

Later, in high school, I played as a strong safety on the football team. We were in a game against one of our big rivals, a powerhouse team that boasted the best field-goal kicker in the district. When that kid took the field that day, we could feel the confidence the rival team had that the kicker was assured an easy three points. Our linebacker coach, Coach Solomon, called me over to him, and told me, "Bobby, I need you to block this kick." I remember I nodded and then began running back to my position. He must not have thought I'd really heard him, because he called me back, and this time he grabbed my face mask and pulled my head close to his so that we were eyeball to eyeball: "*Block that kick.*" I'd never blocked one before or since, but somehow his certainty that I *could* do it was transferred to me. When that kick came, I jumped higher than I'd ever jumped before. I blocked that kick and turned the game around. I learned something that day about the ability a good leader has to inspire his team members to perform at their top potential.

As a green twenty-three-year old managing a team of pipe fitters and welders, most of whom had children older than I was, I saw that the success of my team was my responsibility, the same way it was for my coaches. This wasn't my team's first rodeo. They'd been working on power plants their entire careers, and I could easily see that. They knew what they were doing. But at the end of the day, when the project was wrapped up, it was *my* name that went on the package that validated that everything had been done in accordance to the design specifications approved by the client. I was responsible for that validation, and if my name was going on something, I had to ensure it was done absolutely right. That's why getting the best out of my team mattered so much. How could I inspire them to outperform their best previous efforts, as my coaches had inspired me? This leadership challenge inspired me to read my first book on leadership, Ken Blanchard's *The One Minute Manager*. One of his main points was to "find your people doing things right and praise them." It's motivating to your team. Nothing says you appreciate team members more than paying attention to them, observing and recognizing their strengths. Once we have this knowledge, how can we get team members to improve a task they feel they have already mastered? How do we hone skills to make our team better? Find your team doing things right and praise them; it's motivating. I lived off that one point for many years, and it never let me down.

It took me multiple promotions and years of trial and error as a leader to figure out just what worked. I kept reading and learning and trying out leadership principles and investing in team members. By the time I became a general manager of five power plants, I was getting closer. I began putting my growing list of guiding principles in place within the five plants, and I started to see performance improve. Then, when I became general manager of transmission overseeing the activities and processes of the tristate assets management team and leading three major process improvement teams (safety, human performance, and diversity), I began to use the same leadership system and again saw performance improve. I was fortunate to be promoted to a regional vice president, and I once again relied on this system. I read additional leadership books to hone my leadership skills in order to tweak the model, and again I saw improvement with the thirteen operation centers all vying for the number one, number two, and number three positions. Finally, when I took on my biggest leadership role over fleet services, which encompassed six states and fifty-eight locations, I put these same foundational leadership principles in place—and, once again, we saw performance improve in multiple areas. That's when I knew I had something of value to share with other leaders—proven, battle-tested principles to raise the performance of any team. Whether your workplace is union or nonunion, on the East Coast, West Coast, in the North or South, these principles will work for you. Why? Because people are people, and how we treat them matters!

Here's a question I had to answer for myself: Why would you want to put the effort into building a high-performance team? Doesn't a mediocre or average team get the work done? Well, yes … but a high-performance team does *everything* well. Teamwork and collaboration will improve; problems will get solved faster and better. Morale will soar, and so will productivity. Your team is going to be more willing to follow rules and comply. For those companies that are concerned with safety, you'll see a decrease in accidents and liability claims because team members will look after each other and go the extra mile for each other.

That's what "a high-performing team" looks like, and that's why you as a leader need to commit to this journey of growing your leadership.

WHAT'S YOUR VISION?

As a leader, you need to have a vision of how you want your team to work together and what attitude they will have toward their team members and their work. Many leaders rely on their companies' vision to direct their teams' daily interactions. Many times, the corporate direction doesn't drill down enough to serve that purpose. This is where the leaders must step up with their thoughts and bring these behaviors to life by communicating and demonstrating their own vision.

> **As a leader, you need to have a vision of how you want your team to work together and what attitude they will have toward their team members and their work.**

Clarity around this is critical, because a leader's attitude is contagious. Leaders must come to work with the right attitude in order to bring out the best in the team every day. Leaders have to always be on their game. They can never come in thinking and acting like this is an average, mundane day. If they do, that attitude is projected in their speech, tone of voice, and body language, and it's the attitude their team is going to adopt that day. What's your attitude going to be, leaders? What vibe is your team going to pick up from you? Are they going to sense the winning attitude or mediocrity?

The following three quotes really resonated with me as vision statements. Reading and believing in positive quotes like these prepare me to have a highly impactful day.

1. If better is possible, good is no longer an option.

2. Good is the enemy of great.

3. The only way to succeed at anything is to give it everything.

Now, before you read on, I want you to think about what you hear in these three statements. What do they mean to you? What do they inspire in you?

Take a moment; recast them in your own words. Maybe what you hear is, "good isn't good enough" or that you'll never be great if you settle for "good"—"Am I giving everything I have for the success of my team?" There are so many ways to think about these, and what matters right now is what resonates with *you*. So pick up a pencil, and write down two or three of the thoughts these statements inspire in you, right now, right here in the margins of this book. I want these to be *your* words, words that you repeat to yourself every day until they're part of you. That's the attitude you need to take to work with you every day. That's the vision that will inspire your team.

Your company has entrusted you to lead. Think about that. What do you hear in the word "entrusted"? Write it here in the book, in the margin or above the word "entrusted." What does "entrust" mean? "The company believes in me" might be one thing. "The company has faith in me. I have a responsibility. I've been selected. I've been chosen." All those statements are correct, because they have chosen you. They saw something in you that said you could lead. All that trust has been put in you with the expectations that you will deliver— that whatever those daily needs are, whatever those goals are, you and your team will exceed them. That's what's been entrusted to you. That's the responsibility that each leader holds on their shoulders every single day, the belief and trust that you will deliver. That's a tribute to your perceived capabilities and an obligation to lead and inspire your team to exceed their performance standards and company goals. Don't waste it!

Leaders have impact. "Impact" means how you make your team members feel. This is very important for leaders to understand. We lead people who are our team members who have feelings, emotions, needs for appreciation and respect. Within the feelings and emotions of the team you lead is where their discretionary effort lives. You tap into that, and they're going to the next performance level, so as not to let you down. What you do and how you lead impacts not only your business but also the lives of those you've been entrusted to lead. What are some of the impacts you might have as a leader? Meeting or exceeding goals? Taking on challenges and succeeding? Enabling collaboration and teamwork? Great customer focus? What you see as your impact matters, and how you make team members feel matters. Every day that you come to work, you should show up with the expectation that you're going to make a difference in your team's lives, to get the team one day further on that journey of whatever you're trying to produce, whether it's producing a financial report, making a system, improving a process, or improving supply chain efficiency. Whatever your role is, every day, you should attempt to make a difference in that role, giving your best to get it one day further down the line.

We need leaders and team members who are committed to performing at their top potential, every day, every task. Stop right here; let's take a minute to think about what that statement means to you. Pick up that pencil again, and write your thoughts down now, while they're fresh, because most leaders can't articulate what "top potential" is, and that's why their team can't get there. What does "top potential" look like to you and your team as it pertains to daily tasks? If I were observing the office activities or fieldwork, or if I were on the production floor observing you and your team, what would I see that would inspire me to believe everyone is working at their top potential?

How do we as leaders enable our team members to do that, to bring their very best selves to work and perform every day at the top of their abilities? We have to create an environment that nourishes and encourages that kind of attitude.

Here's the thing: high-potential team members can't perform in a negative environment. They can't perform in a gossipy environment, in a distrusting environment, in a disruptive environment, in an environment where team members don't like each other, where there's hate and discontent, where the tone is negative or rife with complaining, bullying, or teasing. They just won't flourish, and they won't perform. If you've allowed that kind of negativity to infect your team's culture, you'll never see top potential team members emerge. They're afraid to emerge. Top-potential people want to be a part of the solution, but in a poor environment, they're hesitant to step up if they've got others gossiping behind their backs, calling them brown-nosers or suck-ups, or rooting for them to fail. Everybody wants to fit in; nobody wants to be ridiculed in front of their peers.

So many leaders don't get that; they think they can just show up and let the culture manage itself. But that's wrong. You've got to have a vision and belief about what you want that team to do and how you want them to do it. You've got to have expectations about how you're going to treat every member of your team and how you expect them to treat each other. You must show them what giving their best looks like and support them in those efforts. That's what the right environment creates and feeds. Lead by example! If you've got a culture that holds team members back, one focused on negativity—you've got to rid your organization of those destructive, undermining behaviors.

You need team members who believe in the mission, the goals, the vision of being the best. Start with assessing your workforce. Are they on board? Who's not? Who believes and who doesn't? You need to make that distinction; you'll never get the best out of people who don't believe. That person's just there to fill a spot or collect a paycheck.

That person can't help you build an environment that feeds high potential or even adds value to your process.

You need team members who are willing to do what it takes. Once you've identified the believers, the next question is, are they also willing to do what it takes? Transformation isn't easy, and it's going to take the best efforts of everyone on board.

We need leaders who are willing to be the best leaders. Not just average; not just "good enough." Why? Because you're setting the standards, and it's up to you to create and sustain this high-performance environment. That's why the work begins with you, not the team. When they see you doing that, they'll understand it, and they'll be inspired by it. Your extra effort will spur their extra efforts, but it starts with you. Lead by example!

We need leaders who are willing to learn and to apply what they learn. Nobody is born knowing how to build a great culture. You're going to have to learn that, and if you're not willing to put in the effort, you'll never build a high-performance team. I was a sponge for knowledge, eager to learn and eager to apply what I learned. There's always more to know. Don't be afraid to learn, regardless of age and seniority with the company.

I hope you're starting to see by now how important leadership is. If you started this book not sure of the difference between leadership and management, I hope it's starting to click. Management is budgets, org charts, resource management, process improvement, and metrics. Dump all that out of your mind; I'm drilling down to leadership attributes that build and connect with team members and customers. We're human beings, not machines. We crave connection with each other, and we look to leaders for that inspiration and unifying vision. As a leader you've got to be someone worth emulating. Leaders have to be willing to support the culture that feeds that connection and to support the expectations that build team members.

Leadership is a craft. Take a moment here, pick up that pencil, and underline the word "craft." What does that word mean to you? A skill that can be practiced? Something that can be learned? Something that can be improved with work and dedication? All of those are good definitions, and I want you to know that if you want to be a great leader, you'll never stop working on the craft, the skills, of leadership. I'm not going to tell you you've got to read a leadership book every year, but certainly you'd better be reading one at least every couple of years or attending a class or seminar or listening to a leadership podcast. I'm retired from leadership now, but I've never stopped exposing myself to new leadership material, because there's always something to learn, some illumination or insight I haven't considered before. I'm still honing my craft, and you should be too.

Remember this: the behavior of your team/crew is a reflection of you. The attitude of a leader is contagious. This is a huge responsibility and a weighty one. You need to take a moment to consider the gravity of that and what it means to your behavior. When you treat someone disrespectfully, dismissively, unkindly, you're setting a tone, and that tone will be reflected by your team. If I had a problem with a crew or team not performing well, I knew I had a leadership problem, not a crew or team problem. If there was discontent in the ranks, I had a leadership problem. Sometimes I would hear a leader say, "I need better people." No, no, no. I need a better leader. Whatever problem I had, I held the leader responsible, not the employees. That's a heavy load to carry, and not everyone is cut out for it. I can't tell you how many times I've seen people promoted to positions of leadership who just couldn't rise to those expectations, and they ultimately came to me asking to be put back in their old jobs. As a leader, you can't just be there to fill the position and take the check. You're there to lead, and if your team members aren't behaving the way you want them to or performing as you think they should, the buck stops at your desk. Look in the mirror and ask yourself, "Am I demonstrating the right behaviors to my team? Have I created a problem by tolerating poor performance or behavior?" No more blaming others; be self-critical and challenge yourself to be better! Lead by example.

Utility Business Media published a great section in their leadership training titled "Why Managing Attitudes and Behaviors Matter," and this quote says it all:

> Attitude is the tip of the leadership spear and serves as a strong deterrent to apathy. If you lead with a bad attitude, you'll get bad results. If you lead with a good attitude, you'll get good results. What's more, a leader's attitude is contagious. By approaching your role with positivity, you will see your crew respond in kind with more positivity as well. It will also help you extinguish any negatives in the group and keep it (the negative) from spreading and influencing bad behavior amongst your team.

The previous paragraph is one of the most powerful statements about attitude I have ever read. There is so much information in these five sentences that it blew me away the first time I read it. Leaders need to know how impactful, how powerful, their attitudes are. If you absorb this and accept it as truth, marinate on it in your mind, and then act on it, it will add to your self-improvement. You have proof it will work for you in the science that backs up the principle.

No more hiding behind the excuse of "That's just how I am." No more excuses for treating team members badly, because now you know that *your attitude steers the entire team.*

Because this paragraph is so important, let's unpack it sentence by sentence. "Tip of the leadership spear" means your attitude is the first thing people see and feel. Let's say it one more time so you can digest this very important point. Your attitude is the first thing people see and feel. Let's also couple it with "a leader's attitude is contagious." Team members, colleagues, and customers see our attitude; they feel it, and our attitude can be transferred to them. When we get out of the car first thing in the morning at work, the first people we interact with in the parking lot or at the door on our way to our office are impacted by our attitude. Listen to the responsibility here: throughout the day all the people we encounter are impacted by our attitude. We pass it on to others by how we make them feel (good or bad). The key point is that our attitudes are very powerful. Let's examine the next part of the sentence: "leadership serves as a strong deterrent to apathy." We have to first start by defining "apathy," which is a lack of interest, lack of enthusiasm, lack of concern. By having a positive attitude, you can turn apathetic team members into interested, concerned, and enthusiastic ones! How cool is that?

> No more hiding behind the excuse of "That's just how I am." No more excuses for treating team members badly, because now you know that *your attitude steers the entire team.*

The next statement makes a promise and will further the reason why I follow the concept of "everything rises and falls on leadership," and why I hold leadership accountable: "If you lead with a bad attitude, you will get bad results." If you have a team not performing well, there's a leadership problem. On the flip side, if you lead with a good attitude, **you will get good results**.

Now, pay close attention to these next two sentences, because they are a huge gold nugget: "By approaching your role with positivity, you will see your team/crew respond in kind with **more** positivity as well." What this is telling you is that whatever you do to them, you get more of the same back. If you give them positivity, kindness, respect, and appreciation, they will respond in kind (positivity, kindness, respect, and appreciation) with **more** back to you. This should take away any fears you may have that if you're positive toward your team, your team will not respond. In my experience, I can tell you they will respond in kind and will even raise the level of positivity. And what's more, your positive attitude will fight off negative attitudes and keep them from spreading.

When I was the supervisor for mechanical maintenance, one guy didn't like me for whatever reason, but I didn't let that bother me. I tried being extra nice to him, getting him involved, complimenting him where I could, sometimes going overboard to try to win him over. None of these tactics even moved the needle. What did work was focusing on the other guys who wanted to move the shop forward. Encouraged, they came to me with a list of all the things they wanted to see change, including the availability of new training and the chance to take over some of the specialty contractor work. That list grew to ten items. I supported the list and got some guys willing to work on the various items with me, and we were off and running. When that wish list started getting completed, it brought on a surge of energy. Team members were feeling special and appreciated, and morale improved, but this one guy still wanted to say bad things about me and the company. The other team members got tired of him putting me down and saying negative things, so they went and talked to him themselves; they said, "We like what Bob is doing for this shop. No supervisor has ever supported us like this. Get on board or get out." That's what it took to change his attitude, and the negative team member came on board.

Important fact: Your positivity has power. You don't have to fight all the battles. The team will fight for you.

CHAPTER TWO

THE LEADERSHIP PRINCIPLES

'm very excited to share these leadership principles with you. These principles came from trial and error, reading and studying, and from interviews with successful operation centers, plant departments, and maintenance center garages that were on my team. These are not all the leadership principles out there in leadership land, but these have all been battle tested by me throughout my career. Feel free to add your own to the list. I respect your experiences and the successes you've had. If you've found some effective leadership principles, make sure you share them with your peers so that success can be duplicated at your company. Knowledge is power when it's shared. My goal for each of you reading this book is to be a highly successful leader. I want you to have a clear understanding of what works so you have confidence to move your team and company forward. The following principles will provide you with tools to help you move to becoming that highly successful leader.

PRINCIPLE 1: HOW WE TREAT PEOPLE MATTERS

How we treat people matters. Let that sink in a moment, because as simple as it seems, it says a lot. There's a way that we can treat people that will get the best out of them. There's a way we can treat people that will bring the worst out of them. There's also a way to treat people that won't move them in either direction, which is really a negative. But whatever you do, believe that people are impacted by the way you treat them, and believe that how you treat them will affect how well or poor they perform their work—it really will! Relationships matter! I do contract training for a company named Utility Business Media, mentioned in the previous chapter, and another section in their leadership class material discusses relationships: "Relationships are going to happen whether we put forth effort or not. Relationships just happen because people are relational beings." Here's the interesting part; they found that if a leader has a positive relationship with team members, and the expectation that each team member has a positive relationship with the other team members, that team performs better. If the leader puts no effort in building a relationship with the team, a bad relationship will take the place of a potentially good one. Teams evaluate your lack of effort to have a relationship with them and conclude you don't like them or make other negative assumptions about your attitude toward them. So leaders really don't have a choice. Leaders are put in place to get the best out of people, to build high-performing teams. Positive relationships and the manner in which we treat team members to establish that positivity are very important to achieving top performance.

Leaders' development of philosophies on how to treat their teams can come from many sources. They may have had poor experiences or examples of leadership. Some believe that a tough boss gets results or that treating people well feels too much like a personal commitment, and they're not willing to give that much of themselves. Some are afraid of getting too close to their teams, assuming they could be manipulated in the future, so they keep their distance, but it's a wrong assumption. Strong relationships build strong teams, which sets the stage for a great work environment, one that's going to enable the people on your team to perform at their highest potential.

Give your team your best, and they will give you their best. John Maxwell says in his book *Becoming a Person of Influence* that one of his leadership principles is, "Give with no strings attached." When I first read that, the idea of giving freely resonated powerfully with me. It's significant because it goes against what humans in relationships are naturally going to expect: that if we give something, we're going to get something, because relationships are supposed to be transactional two-way streets. We don't want to get shortchanged. I can understand that, and I can see how team members could be concerned. But I can tell you that I've practiced this idea of giving with no strings attached, and it's been very, very powerful—and you won't get shortchanged.

People sense when you support them—it connects them, it inspires them, and they respond by doing their best for you. Another quote from John Maxwell summarizes what I mean here: "Treat a person the way they are, and you make them worse, but treat them as you want them to be and you make them great." Let that sink in. Whenever I took over a team, I always said positive things about them, whether it was true at the time or not. I wanted it to be true at some time in the future, so I called it out now. Call out what you want them to aspire to, and most will get there. I'll share more of this concept in principle number five.

Let me share some examples of giving with no strings attached; you decide if I got shortchanged. This example is regarding two team members I hired. One was a young lady who was just phenomenal. When we sat down together for her first evaluation after she'd worked with me for about a year, I let her know: "You really have something special. When I watch you work, when I watch you interact with people, hear your questions, see your insight, your intellect, your willingness it's clear to me that you've got something special. And you are going to be outstanding. You're going to be a great leader in whatever position you decide to pursue." I did everything I could to help her prove me right, gave her as many opportunities as I could, and continued to be her cheerleader and advocate in succession planning meetings.

At that time, she had been hired to lead my work management area. She stayed on my team for two and a half years and performed extremely well before getting her next promotion. I had the pleasure of being instrumental in helping her get that next stretch assignment. Then, further down the road after I became a regional vice president, her name came up for a promotion to regional vice president, and I was ecstatic. It's so rewarding when you see someone deserving, to whom you've given "no strings attached" support, rise in the work environment to become a peer.

A similar thing happened with a gifted young man whom I hired. I welcomed him to the team and became genuinely invested in him: his interests, his beliefs, and his family, and the things that brought him joy. When you give someone the opportunity to work in an area that they love, you know they're going to be outstanding. I worked with him to understand his unique strengths and to help him think about where he wanted to go, and I supported him in growing his talents. He, too, performed very well and helped our region be successful. Down the road he also was promoted to a regional vice president—another deserving team member, with whom I received considerable satisfaction with "no strings attached."

Both of them ultimately became senior VPs, and deservedly so. I can remember someone asking me if that bothered me that I'd stayed a regional VP while these two former teammates had moved on to senior VP roles. I was able to honestly answer, "Absolutely not." I knew when they came into my team that they had something special, something that was really going to accelerate their careers and move them vertically. I was happy to just have been a part of that and watch them soar and do great things. Their success helped me validate the tenets I applied when mentoring them, and I used those lessons with others.

Did I get shortchanged?

How we treat people matters!

PRINCIPLE 2: YOU MUST LIKE PEOPLE

If you're a leader and you do not like people, you must get out of leadership. There is no way in the world you're ever going to make the personal connections you need in order to get the best out of team members. I'll never forget hearing one of my supervisors say, "This would be a great job if it wasn't for the people." He could see from my expression that he'd shocked and disappointed me. I had to challenge him on that statement because I had discussed how I wanted our employees treated, and if he couldn't live up to that expectation, I couldn't have him on the team. Leadership is all about the people—it's connecting, inspiring, building people up, trusting, empowering, and communicating with your team.

General Colin Powell once said, "The day the soldiers stop bringing you their problems is the day you stopped leading them. They have either lost confidence that you can help them or concluded that you do not care. Either case is a failure of leadership." I couldn't agree more. Caring for people is essential if you're going to be effective in a leadership role.

PRINCIPLE 3: YOU CAN'T HAVE EXCELLENCE WITHOUT GREAT TOGETHERNESS AND GREAT TEAMWORK

This is an idea I adopted from Lou Holtz's *Do Right* video, which I've shared with every one of my leadership teams since I first experienced it. Holtz references togetherness in the video, a term which has struck me most powerfully. I love it; it's such a warm word, and a great way of thinking about your relationships in your team and the relationship they have for each other.

Thinking about teamwork as togetherness elevates the value of each and every person on the team. That's very, very important, because so often I see teams effectively devaluing themselves and others by measuring their importance against others on the organizational chart: from the top, the CEO, senior leaders, GMs, plant managers, supervisors, and finally themselves at the bottom. That leads to belittling self-definitions that start with "Well, I'm just …" as in "I'm just a mechanic"; "I'm just an electrician"; "I'm just in the finance group"; "I'm just in the auditing group." When team members use the org chart like a measuring stick to tell them what they're worth, their job can seem very far removed from those who society tells us are important.

The truth is that we need everyone on the team working in perfect alignment to be excellent. No matter how big the challenge is, that level of excellence can only be gained if everyone feels valued and is committed to giving their best and giving their all. When that happens, when everyone feels that charge of energy that hits us when we see ourselves as an important part of the greater effort, somewhere in that nucleus of energy, you're going to find excellence. I love it when Lou Holtz says, "Get people to believe in themselves," because when you do that, those people will set higher goals for themselves. I'm a believer in and a witness to the truth of his words. Over my career, I sponsored and facilitated many company-wide teams covering three regions and six states—teams that supported process improvement, diversity, safety, human performance, and work management. As I integrated my high level of energy and passion, it caught on like wildfire. That energy facilitated the team's development of charters, where we defined our roles and responsibilities, our vision, and mission.

This part of the process is where the team sees the value in the team, and they become excited to be a part of this initiative. The next part involves the creation of the subteams. The subteam is where the action begins. These teams bring the charter alive with initiatives that, when accomplished, will move the needle. Once these teams start scheduling meetings, conference calls, and completing tasks, that's when the belief in themselves is established, and then they want to do more because they see their efforts making a positive difference. The next round of initiatives are more challenging than the first because the team is confident, and they believe in themselves as a team.

> **You can't have excellence without great togetherness and great teamwork.**

PRINCIPLE 4: WE CAN'T CHANGE PEOPLE; PEOPLE CHANGE THEMSELVES IF THEY'RE WILLING

This one's huge, bigger than big. As leaders, it's our responsibility to provide great leadership skills, principles, expectations, and culture. We can use all those qualities and traits as influence to help bring about an individual's change, but the final choice is up to the individual. Leaders don't own their team members' personal decisions. If team members don't decide to embrace the company's and team's vision and goals, leadership is faced with a decision of its own. Remember, part of their job description and how they earn their pay is to help the company move forward and improve to meet customer needs. If team members no longer want to do that, we have a "culture fit" problem.

To understand this principle, you first have to understand the type of personality I'm talking about. This is the kind of person whom some organizations refer to as a "hardliner." A hardliner is someone whose heels are dug in. A person who doesn't like change and who always complains when it's introduced. A person who, no matter what the new change is—be it a process, a new tool, a new uniform, whatever it is—has a knee-jerk response of resistance. They're the ones with the reliably negative attitude, the headshakers and naysayers. They come in all shapes, sizes, and demographics, but what they all have in common is that "glass half empty" attitude, which effectively stifles innovative thinking, smart risk taking, and progress.

Early in my leadership career, I would expend a lot of time on these hardliners, trying to get them on board, and, to some extent, I measured my leadership effectiveness by whether or not I succeeded. Now, of course I had team members who were doing great things, but it never felt like a win to me if I couldn't get everyone on board and moving in the same direction. But the hardliners were tough to convert—in fact, very often impossible. Still, it troubled me because I believed that somehow, I *could* win them over, if I just knew the right way to go about it.

I finally got free of this belief in 1997 when I was part of the company's diversity and inclusion development team, and we were on a video conference call with Allstate Insurance up in New York. It was a company at that time that was known for having a very good leadership accountability plan and process. I asked their team, "How do you handle hardliners?" because that was very much on my mind at the time.

The answer was so fluid and perfect; I've never forgotten it.

"That's simple, Bob," he began.

I was thinking, "Simple? I'm struggling!"

But he continued, "This is what we do. We remediate them twice … "

I understood what "remediate" meant: whatever particular task we were trying to get these folks to learn, if they didn't show the aptitude that we expected after training, we put them through the class again and then put them back out there. If they still didn't get it, we remediated them again. That's a lot of time and money spent on remediating people with the same message, expecting them to get it and for it to finally click.

He continued, " … and after two remediations, if they don't get it or catch on, then we stamp their folder 'Unwilling.'"

Unwilling! Talk about a light bulb moment! When I heard that word, it was like an epiphany. There was no way that I could get these folks to change if they didn't want to, if they were unwilling. No matter how much time I spent with them, if they themselves lacked the will to alter their attitudes, they would never do so, and it was a waste of my effort. Taking in that concept at that moment changed my view completely. It was liberating.

When I went back to the office that day, I was determined to put my focus on the positive people, the ones who *did* get it, who wanted to give their best, and it made all the difference. When my focus was on the negative people, coddling them and trying to get them involved, that attitude just handed them more power to push their negativity onto the organization. Once I started focusing on the positive team members, the team moved forward. We started accomplishing things on their list: new training, new opportunities to take over work, improving our facilities, and doing more than upper management had thought we were capable of, because once that "positivity" attitude took hold, we were unstoppable. Now, we still extended great leadership attributes toward the hardliners, but we no longer focused on their attitude or allowed their attitude to drive the team's emotions and therefore its progress.

Yes, as a leader, you can influence someone, but you can't make them change. They have to want to change. Some people will tell you they just can't change, but we know that's a farce, because we've seen that people can change as quickly as they want to once they decide that it is going to benefit them. I had a team member on my team at one point who flatly refused to learn an upgraded process that required him to push two additional keys on the computer to generate a work order. He insisted to me he couldn't do it; he claimed that he just didn't have any skills—bear in mind, he was already using the computer and pushing several keys right then. But when I cornered him and started asking him about his ability to use a smartphone, or to visit with his grandkids on Skype, or about the computer systems that set up his new pickup truck, it was very evident to me that this was an intelligent team member who understood all of these things very well, despite his claims that he couldn't. Learning how to use those two keys ultimately benefitted him, so he adopted their use, and that benefited me and negated the whole notion that he wasn't smart enough or capable of learning how to push a few more keys to learn a new work management process. People can change, and they will change when they see a benefit to themselves.

My advice is that when you find yourself with a hardliner on your team, don't waste a lot of time with them. Love them, respect them, and treat them as valued team members, but don't expend a lot of effort trying to get them involved. Work with the team members who are committed and who've proven their commitment by being part of the solutions, and who are excited about moving the team forward. Work with those team members, and watch the team grow and improve. Sometimes they can change the attitude and disruptive behavior of the hardliner. When the hardliner sees their teammates having fun and making accomplishments, they may want to be involved. Also, remind the hardliner that it's in their job description to help the company move forward and improve to meet team, company, and customer needs. If they no longer want to do that, we have a "culture fit" problem. Be ready to have a critical conversation about what other departments the hardliner would like to consider if they're no longer happy in their current team. Sometimes the change is what they want. Some employees need a change, and the right change brings out the best in them. If that doesn't work, be ready to elevate the conversation to retirement or the fact that this may no longer be the right company for them. We cannot allow hardliners' negative behaviors to sabotage our progress.

Change the people or change the people!

PRINCIPLE 5: START OUT RIGHT BY BELIEVING IN PEOPLE

Belief is one of the most powerful tools we have as leaders. When people feel their leader believes in them, they can and will do great things; it lifts them up and makes those great things possible. I told the story earlier about the field goal I blocked in a playoff game. That would never have happened had Coach Solomon not made it clear that he believed I could succeed and expected me to succeed. When he saw that I didn't have the right look in my eye, that look of confidence, he called me back, grabbed my face mask, pulled me in eyeball to eyeball, and told me, "Block that kick. You can do it." When I got out there on that field, I blocked the kick, but I don't think I could have done it without that infusion of confidence that my coach gave me in the moment I needed it most.

So many team members are crippled with self-doubt and just don't believe that they're capable of going the distance. But once they see someone they respect who believes in them and feels that their strengths add value to the team, they rise in their own estimation, and they'll go above and beyond to justify that leader's faith in them. That holds true, regardless of their position.

Team members need to believe in each other, too, and share and show that faith. That's got to be part of your expectations for how team members treat each other. That kind of supportive thinking spreads like wildfire, and it starts with you.

I'd start with sending out positive emails to my team: simple things like "Good morning to the best leaders in the utility industry." I'd look for every opportunity to say positive things. I sent birthday cards to the team members and took the time to write in them myself. I used phrases like "You're awesome" or "You're the man (or woman)!" I drew smiley faces and large exclamation points. In group emails, I'd always include positive things about the team and how great they were at the things that they did—all this to let them know that I believed in them and cared about them.

As a leader, you can be a catalyst for creating a movement that touches people's lives—one that energizes people to create a culture where it's okay for us to praise each other, to say good things to each other, and to believe in each other. Be that positive leader; make sure that every person on your new team knows that's who you are from day one. Let them know that you respect them, that you trust them, and that you believe in them.

And this is the important part: they shouldn't have to earn it. You simply give it to them.

A lot of us grew up thinking that people had to somehow earn our trust, but what does that mean in practice, really? I've often wondered about that. When I became the general manager over fifty-eight locations spread over six states, I realized that it would be impossible for every one of those people to "earn" my trust. How could I hope to be with each member of my team at a point where I would observe them doing something that would make me deem them trustworthy, or worthy of respect? Clearly, it was a ridiculous idea.

So I let people know the first day I meet them, "I respect you right now. I don't know you well because I just met you, but I respect you because you're here to work, trying to take care of your family, trying to do the best you can. That trust is yours to lose, but right now I trust you. I think you're a good person, I like you, and I'm looking forward to working with you. I think you're a winner because you come day in day out, year after year, and give your best." When you let people know that's how you feel, it calms them down, because of course it's stressful to have a new boss coming in. They're wondering how you are going to treat them, or how you'll respond to them, and by letting them know that you trust them from day one, you've reassured them and they can relax; they have no reason not to like and trust you back. It's natural.

You've got to actually say the words, not just assume they'll get it without being told. You've got to show them with your actions, too, because those have to match your words, and as a new leader, the team will be watching you to see if you mean what you say. This goes back to principle one—how you treat people matters. When people realize you're sincere, you'll unlock something in them that's just unbelievable. You won't believe how hard they'll work to justify that trust and respect. You make people feel special, you make people feel like winners, and they'll move heaven and earth to prove you right.

Let's finish this principle off with a five-day leadership challenge that I want you to try: every morning for five days, when you walk into the office in the morning, you greet whomever you can. It can be anyone, but make sure you start with your own team members. Shake their hands and make good eye contact (the eye contact is very important because that's how we transfer belief), and tell them something good, like "You're a leader, and you can make a difference. I'm so glad that you're on the team."

Now, that seems like a small thing (and in terms of effort on your part, it really is), but it has a ripple effect that will pass through your whole team. This five-day challenge will be contagious, because when your people feel that belief you have in them, they're naturally going to pass that along to the next person. It's a small thing that can make a big difference. John Maxwell says, "Believe in people before they prove themselves." I'm a witness that it works.

PRINCIPLE 6: SAY POSITIVE THINGS THAT BUILD TEAM MEMBERS UP

I love the word "positive." What I don't love is what so many of us have allowed to come into our workplaces: the poisonous culture of office gossip and negativity. It's so easy to fall into it, and so tough to root out, but we all know it's toxic. Life is tough for all of us; each one of us will get kicked in the teeth by life. When we come to work, let's not do it to each other. Let's create a culture full of love, value, respect, and appreciation.

When I speak to groups, I always say, "Let's go back to what Mom taught us. What did Mom say? If you don't have anything good to say about anybody … " and I stop and look out at the group. And it doesn't matter what part of the country I'm in, or whether it's a group of two hundred or a group of eight hundred—they all finish the sentence for me: " … don't say anything at all!" Mom was right about that, and we all know it. Yet when we become adults, we somehow think that we can now talk trash about other team members and put them down. We forget what Mom told us, and that's bad.

As a leader, it's your responsibility to set a higher standard. Start making a point of saying positive things about people. Reject the temptation to gossip, and make sure that those working with you understand there's no place for that. There's plenty of good going on in each of our lives; it's not a challenge to find something upbeat and good to say about each other. Make the effort to comment on the strengths that you see others show at work; take an interest in others' hobbies. Look for the good in each person, and find an opportunity to mention it. It makes a better work environment; it makes people feel cared for, appreciated, and esteemed, and that impacts how they'll work for you and with each other. It changes the whole atmosphere for the better.

PRINCIPLE 7: FIND PEOPLE DOING THINGS RIGHT AND PRAISE THEM

This came from Ken Blanchard's book *The One Minute Manager*, the first leadership book I read. Find people doing things the right way, and praise them. People do more right things than wrong. Get out there and observe, look for those things they do right, and then praise them. If you don't have any praise left in your heart for your team, if you can't find anything to admire in them or their work, then it's probably time for you to get out of leadership. People love to work where they're appreciated. They are thankful to be in an environment that's free of team members putting others down, free from backbiting, negativity, complaining, self-proclaimed spokes-people, bullies, and teasers. High performance people can't work in a negative atmosphere.

When you find people doing things right and you praise them, it's motivating. When you can identify people's strengths and allow them to demonstrate them, it inspires them. It's an opportunity to delegate, as well as an opportunity for you as a leader to share your belief in them, to empower them by expressing that belief, and by setting the expectation to the group that it's okay to say great things about each other, it's okay to make each other happy at work. That kind of unwavering support gets attention, and it gets copied. When people see you as their leader modeling that kind of behavior, they respond in kind. If that's not the atmosphere in your workplace now, fix it.

PRINCIPLE 8: DON'T HAVE FAVORITES AT WORK

I can see that look on your face as you read this one, but please, bear with me. I get it—it's natural for us as people to be drawn to those who have the same kinds of hobbies and interests that we do. I remember early on in my bodybuilding career, I had a couple of team members at the office who worked out and shared that interest. I also love cars, and I had a couple of other team members who liked cars also. So when I would come in, my intention was to make the time to speak to everyone there and to get around to everybody on my team. But where I'd tend to stop was with the guys who had the same interests as I did: the bodybuilders and the car guys. It's so easy to get wrapped up in the people who have the same hobbies you do, but it's not fair. As leaders, we know that our team members are watching us all the time and evaluating our behavior. When they see us enjoying each team members' interests and gifts, they will do the same, and that's what we want—everybody on the team getting to know each other, appreciating each other, building a positive relationship with each other.

That's why, as a leader, you can't afford to have favorites, because you don't want to create distance between or isolate team members. In order to have the high-performing culture that will get the best out of all team members, leaders must value everyone on the team. Spend time with everybody on your team, treat them all well, help each one of them to succeed, and give everyone an opportunity to shine.

> **People work best for and with those who make them feel good about themselves.**

PRINCIPLE 9: HELP PEOPLE GET WHAT THEY WANT, AND THEY'LL HELP YOU GET WHAT YOU WANT

That idea behind this principle came from watching Lou Holtz's *Do Right* video that I mentioned in principle 3. The first time I heard "Help people get what they want, and they'll help you get what you want," I pondered over what it meant, and applying it in many of my leadership roles helped me to see how powerful the statement is. I started calling it a leadership principle.

We have to start by asking ourselves: What are the concrete, tangible things that matter to our team members in their work life, family life, and career life? Now, consider what you could do as their leader that would improve each of their lives in these three critical areas. How could you benefit a team member's work, family, and career life?

I don't expect you to know the answers yet. But what this principle is intended to do is to encourage you to pay closer attention to your team than you probably are now and ask each of them individually and in the group the following questions, which enabled me to help provide the opportunities for my teams to grow and become significant among their peers:

- ➡ "How do we make our team/department better?"

- ➡ "What training, tools, and processes do we need to make us better?"

- ➡ "Are there any work skills we could learn and apply that would save the company money?"

- ➡ "What's the condition of our facilities? Does everything work? Is it equal to other departments?"

→ "Where are our salaries? Are we being paid the same as others who do what we do?"

→ "What could we do to make this workplace and your job here more pleasant or more meaningful?"

→ "What can I do for you?"

→ "Where do you want to go with your career?"

→ "What's going on in your family [new baby, aging or sick parents, significant other working a different shift, children in travel sports, college-age children looking for an internship, etc.] that I can help you with, within company policy?"

I did this when I was a mechanical maintenance supervisor, and it worked so well, I did it in other areas I lead. Get the team together, and make a list of things that come up in the questions above. If there are many items, try to consolidate the items and prioritize so you can go for the heavy hitters in the first round. They should be the items that, once completed, will build great team spirit and togetherness. Solicited volunteers from the team who are passionate about the various topics will help lead the initiative. There's no way the leader can and should own all the items on the list. Plus, the team needs to show their commitment and own their ideas.

At the shop, my team wanted to take over the fire protection inspection. We had previously hired outside experts to do those inspections, but the team wanted that work. I got one of my trainers to come up with the curriculum to teach and qualify our guys to do it. Now we could do the fire inspections at the plant, increasing our value and saving money for the plant. That led to more training for other specialty areas, giving my team increased expertise and greater responsibilities. They wanted an ice cream machine and a hot dog roller too. And you know what? We got them, and it made the shop a fun place. Working on these initiatives really raised the level of energy and commitment in the shop. The team had input and they'd been heard, and they were invested in the outcomes. That gave those training programs added credibility as well, and if someone complained about it, the response from the shop was, "Hey, that's not management's idea, that was my idea, and I support it." That level of ownership cut out all the nonsense and complaining that usually follows new initiatives in the workplace. Because they were invested in the new initiatives, they were advocates.

When I took over fleet services, I visited all fifty-eight locations. I made a list of several poor conditions I observed in some of these places. We began to fix air conditioners that had been broken for a long time, replacing poor lighting, upgrading equipment for all maintenance garages (not just the ones that were most visible), painted walls, and got uniforms for those who were wearing their own clothes when other departments had company uniforms. We raised the supervisors' salaries to match the other departments.

As those things started happening, the people who were the beneficiaries of these improvements built up a momentum that was just unstoppable; it was not just in those specific tasks, but our overall performance also went up a couple of notches. Why? Because team members were happy and engaged. With that level of engagement, your teams aren't trying to make mistakes—they're trying to catch mistakes. They're trying to help you look good because you helped them.

As I continued to get more responsibilities, I would use that level of influence to help my team. While I served as regional vice president, I did a lot of things in the community, serving on the boards of local colleges. When I overhear my employees talking about how hard it was to get registered or problems their kids were having at these colleges, I was able to use my influence to look into those problems and resolve them for their family members. That's powerful, because people are grateful when you help their families out. One of my team members came to me to thank me for helping his daughter get a roommate situation straightened out and asked me, "How did you know about that?" I explained that I'd overheard someone mention she was having problems at one of the schools to which I was connected; I wasn't going to let that happen, so I'd taken the liberty of making a phone call about it, and I'd asked them to look into it. The next thing we knew, the problem had been solved.

Whenever I'd hear that someone on my team had a family member in the hospital, I'd be sure to send them a little gift basket, just to let them know that we were thinking about them and praying for them. When your people know you're going out of your way to extend that love and care for their family, it's powerful. When you do those kinds of things for your team members, they bring back an immeasurable level of commitment to you as a leader because they appreciate the care that you've shown for them and their family. For most of us, nothing is more important than our loved ones, and nothing is more stressful than seeing someone you love sick or having problems. As a leader, knowing what matters to your team and making the effort to show that you care are tremendous displays of team loyalty.

PRINCIPLE 10: GET TO KNOW EACH TEAM MEMBER PERSONALLY

You've probably noticed a lot of these principles tie into each other. Getting to know each team member personally all goes back to building trust and relationships, all of which requires effort on your part. Have a standard set of questions you ask each employee: Where were you born and raised? What are your hobbies? Tell me about your family. What do you like to do at work? What are your strengths? The better you know your team as individuals, the more connected they feel, and you can leverage those strengths to help the team improve.

Make every interaction with your team members memorable. When I oversaw those five power plants, I had a lot of people—six or seven hundred—working on my teams. I didn't know everybody's name, but whenever someone approached me to start a conversation, I made sure to ask their name and to fully engage in that conversation, asking questions and reacting to the answers. I assure you, when they walked away from me, they felt loved, they felt respected and valued, and they knew they'd been heard.

When I'd run into an employee out in the community with their family, I would make it a point to tell their family what a valuable worker they were and how we couldn't do without them on the team, that their dad or their son, daughter, or significant other was a great person. It might sound trivial, but I promise you, it moves mountains. When you make the effort to get to know team members personally, they will work for you. Because you've said nice things about them, team members really want to do whatever it takes to make you look good.

I've talked in this chapter about the principles a leader must apply in order to help their teams be their best. In the next chapter, we'll turn the table and take a long look at what attributes you, the leader, need to bring to the table and have an expectation that the team demonstrates the attributes toward each other.

CHAPTER THREE

LEADERSHIP ATTRIBUTES

Treat a person as they appear to be and you make them worse.
But treat a person as if they already were what they potentially
could be, and you make them what they should be.

—Johann Wolfgang von Goethe

These attributes are not a comprehensive list of all the necessary leadership attributes. They are, however, the ones I've found to be the most powerful. These attributes must exist in you and your team members. The key is that you as the leader must take the initiative to be the first to begin to demonstrate these attributes toward your team. Remember, as John Maxwell said, "Everything rises and falls on leadership." Your team members are a reflection of you; a leader's attitude is contagious. By demonstrating these attributes toward the team, the team will learn your expectations for what these attributes look like in their daily work lives, and they'll know they're expected and encouraged to treat each other the same way too.

ATTRIBUTE 1: VALUING OTHERS

I came across the idea of value back around 1997 when I volunteered to join the company's diversity team. The idea of workplace diversity was starting to get traction around that time, and the company had put together a team to research the topic and to bring that information back. As we started doing more sessions around diversity, the word "value" came up. Employees need to feel valued, and as leaders we need to know how to make them feel that way. The more we looked at that idea, the more it seemed to me to be an important trait for all leaders, because when we value team members, we talk to them and respond to them differently, and that posture is what impacts team members (how we make them feel).

To understand value, let's stop a moment and call to mind a person you really value. Someone in your personal life—your child, a parent, or grandparents, your spouse if you're married, perhaps a special coach or teacher—whoever it is, think about that one person you value the most.

Now that you've got a picture of that person in your mind, tell me: If that person came into the room right now, what would be your physical reaction? This is key, your physical response, your body language.

You're probably thinking, "I would smile. My eyes would light up; I'd jump up to go and greet them." That body language says it all—you value that person, you recognize that person as important and loved, and you're delighted to see them. "I value you" is what you need to project to every person—*every person*—on your team, and you've got to get good at it. And when I say, "Get good at it," I don't want you to think you're going to get good at it in order to manipulate your team. No, you're going to get good at it so you're able to *connect* with your team and make them feel valuable to the team and to the company. When you see them on a daily basis, your face is going to light up, you're going to smile at them, you're going to greet them, you're going to go over to talk with them, and you're going to make that personal contact. You're going to interact with them just like you would with someone that you value personally.

When you get to where you can demonstrate value toward each team member and make them feel valued, they will want to reciprocate, and they'll strive to please you.

ATTRIBUTE 2: LOVE

The love I'm talking about here regarding leadership is that genuine look-after-someone kind of love. This is the love that expresses genuine concern and care for your team's well-being. I've talked a lot about this in previous chapters, so I won't drag it out. Look out for them, look after them, consider them, and approach them with love. I always tell folks, if you want to be approachable, you have to approach them. It's not good enough just to say, "I'm approachable." You have to make the first step. When you approach them—which makes you approachable, because now you're engaging them in conversation and listening to them—you're creating that feeling of love and of caring with the interest you show.

ATTRIBUTE 3: HAPPINESS

"Happy" was a big thing in the '60s, '70s, and '80s. I can remember when I was growing up, our family loved to go to the big company picnics that my dad's employers would throw. Those were such fun events for my sister and me. They were held at the local amusement park or some other big park, and we would sit and watch our dad play softball with his coworkers. The moms and wives all talked together; there were sack races and water activities for the kids.

But in the '90s and early 2000s, corporate America started to lose "happy." Those big picnics, the Christmas parties, the amusement park days, the softball teams—companies stopped sponsoring those kinds of get-togethers due to shrinking budgets. Those decades became what I now refer to as the "process years," where businesses were taking the focus off employees and putting it onto developing processes. We got really good at creating efficient processes, which led to employees become more or less interchangeable and expendable, since anyone could do a given job as long as they followed the process. We made a mistake with that, because we lost touch with the uniqueness of employees and what they brought to their jobs. This attribute is linked to some of the previous principles we discussed in the last chapter, where we discussed knowing your team members' strengths. By applying these processes and interchangeability, we lose the ability to leverage those strengths, and the team member no longer feels a sense of uniqueness. Tap into those strengths—not to the point where a team member feels they are the go-to for every undesirable task, but to the point where they feel respected and valued and they are *happy* they were given the opportunity to both be recognized and to excel.

Diversity programs started to bring happy back with the focus on the needs of the employee. I believe in happy. I've found that a happy team will do an outstanding job. As I've mentioned previously, when team members can come to work and really just be themselves, they're happy about that. When team members know that the work culture is free of the kinds of behaviors that destroy team performance, they're happy. When team members know they're respected, appreciated, valued, and loved, they're happy. I tell teams that life is tough, and every one of us will get kicked in the teeth by life at some point. Parents and other loved ones will pass on, there will be a cancer diagnosis or some other serious illness, accidents will happen, or kids will make poor decisions. But we're not going to inflict hurt or trouble on each other at work. Let's make work a hassle-free zone so we can be here to support each other as we face life's problems. I guarantee you, when you make your team feel happy and have the expectation that the team treats each other that way, you will see improvement in collaboration, productivity, teamwork, and their willingness and desire to take on new challenges.

> I guarantee you, when you make your team feel happy and have the expectation that the team treats each other that way, you will see improvement in collaboration, productivity, teamwork, and their willingness and desire to take on new challenges.

ATTRIBUTE 4: RESPECT

We throw the word "respect" around a lot. Respect each other, follow the golden rule (or better yet, the platinum rule), and treat team members the way they want to be treated. It's important to keep respect paramount in terms of our relations with others, giving them not just what I refer to as a carte blanche respect, but respect for them as team members and as individuals. When someone shares something personal with you about their faith, culture, family, or beliefs those are things that you need to remember to honor in your relations with them going forward. That shows them that you hold a deep respect for them, and when team members are respected, they will respect you and others team members in return. A leader's attitude is contagious.

ATTRIBUTE 5: ENGAGEMENT

What does it mean to engage people? It's simply to find their strengths, what they like to do and what they want to do. A great time for this is during your monthly one-on-ones, performance evaluation times, or daily observations of finding them doing things right. Dedicate some of that time to talking just about the person, their concerns, their ideas, and their thoughts for improvement. Make sure you're writing it down so that together, you can create a personal developmental plan for each team member. Also let your team know that as special assignments come up, you'll be assigning them based on alphabetical order to ensure everyone gets a chance to shine.

Let them know, too, that they won't be alone. After you give them an assignment, you and the team will be there to support them so they can be successful. This is a powerful gesture—everybody helping each other to be successful. When we all have each other's backs, it gives everyone confidence and promotes teamwork.

For leaders with technical teams who work in the field, your approach should be similar in terms of meeting with your team members to identify their strengths. The only difference is that during your prejob brief or beginning-of-the-day planning meeting, you'll want to start letting each team member have an opportunity to speak, not just the foreman. Everyone takes a turn at running the planning meeting and takes a turn addressing the team daily on what their role is in completing the job, their progress, obstacles, and what the team can do to support them. This builds self-esteem in all positions in the field, no matter what the job classification.

ATTRIBUTE 6: APPRECIATION

I just love the word "appreciate"; I love how it sounds, and I love the attitude toward the people it describes—being appreciative. It starts with how we make people feel.

Those who know me know that I love dogs. I volunteer every Saturday at our local dog shelter, the Charlotte Mecklenburg Animal Shelter. We train these dogs, we bathe them, we exercise them, and we socialize with them, because this is a shelter for stray dogs and owner-surrender dogs, and it's our job to get them ready to be adopted. I love the body language of a dog. When you come into a room and a dog who knows you is there, their body language is, "Hey! There you are! I was looking for you." It doesn't matter if they've just seen you a minute before; they come up, and they love on you. If you start to head for another room, their body language is, "Where're you going? I'll go with you. And I'll just sit in there with you while you do whatever you do, but I just want to be around you." That kind of openhearted, unconditional appreciation is what we need to show our team members.

How can we show our appreciation for our team members? By being around them, knowing them, and providing training, mentoring, and whatever else they need to be successful. Say positive things that build them up. Find them doing things right, and praise them publicly so the rest of the team learns each other's strengths and can celebrate their excellence. In meetings or in regular conversation, make it a point to say, "Thank you so much; that's a great point.

> **When you see a team member whose actions or attitude are making a positive difference, say it. Don't be afraid to show them that appreciation and reinforce the culture you want.**

Thank you for bringing that up. I appreciate the way that you always use great graphs in your presentations," or "I overheard you talking to one of the teammates, and I love what you said to that teammate." When you see a team member whose actions or attitude are making a positive difference, say it. Don't be afraid to show them that appreciation and reinforce the culture you want.

ATTRIBUTE 7: UNDERSTANDING

The importance of making others feel understood is something I learned through Pastor Gary Chapman, the author of *The Five Love Languages*. He talks about listening with your eyes. The goal of listening with your eyes is to pay attention to how your team member feels about the topic they're discussing with you. When you can call out an emotion that you detected in their conversation like, "I see that upset you," or "You look happy about that," and your team member validates your perception by saying, "Yes, I do feel that way," at that point your team member feels deeply understood. Note that when people feel deeply understood by you, they will go overboard to understand you.

Once I comprehended the power of understanding and listening with my eyes, I changed the whole configuration of my office. My office had a large conference room attached to it, with a big, long table. When my direct reports would come in, we'd go in there to meet. But once the importance of listening with my eyes was clear to me, I wanted a smaller table for those meetings. We kept the big one for large groups, but for one-on-one meetings, now we meet around a two-person table so that we can sit closer together and facing each other. I hate doing these kinds of meetings from across my desk; it just feels like such a cheap power play, an "I'm in charge; you're not" kind of thing. Some people may not see it that way, but I think they feel it, even if they're not conscious of it. I don't want that, or the big conference table, because we wind up being too far apart both physically and mentally.

Here's another thing that's very important, when you're practicing listening with your eyes, *get away from your electronics*. That's another good reason not to sit at your desk; when you're sitting at your desk and someone's sitting across from you, your phone and computer are directly in between the two of you, and we're all essentially trained to look down at our phones when we hear a *zzz-zzz*, or up at our computer screens when we hear a *ding*. When people have something to share with you and you start the conversation off decently but that *zzz-zzz* or that *ding* happens and you look away from them, you've shattered their moment and made them feel unimportant.

Something for you to practice: Get into the habit of taking notes as you listen. I always have a pad and pen, so I can have the information that I need to follow up on for whomever I'm meeting with. Never, never, never trust that you will remember, because it will come back to bite you. When I was at the plant, one of my guys shared something in our meeting that he wanted me to look into, something that was pretty important to him. I told him, "I'll do it." But you know how it goes; it was probably eight thirty in the morning, and then I didn't see him for a couple of days. I had all the good intentions in the world of getting back to it, but sure enough, I forgot. I trusted that I would remember, and that's the worst thing we can do.

When you forget to follow up, inevitably you will see the team member two or three days later, and as they approach you, you can see it in their eyes, that anticipation: "Did you look into that? Do you have anything for me?" And there you are, stuck, saying, "I forgot." Right at that moment, when they realize that you forgot, you can actually see their body react; they'll break eye contact, their shoulders will go down. They're visibly disappointed, and at that point, all you can do is apologize—and I mean, go overboard with the apologies. "Man, I tell you what; I'm really sorry." Get that person to look up at you. "I'm just so sorry. I know you told me, and I had every intention;

I just completely forgot. Please accept my apologies, and if you give me another chance, I'll look into it right now."

Don't be that guy. Get yourself a little notebook you can keep in your pocket or bag, so when people share things with you, you can write them down. I can't tell you how helpful it is or how much it wins people over, not only when they see you taking the time to write down their concerns, but also when you actually follow through and look into whatever it was you said you'd check on, or have the information for them when you see them. This further supports and leverages our discussion in attribute 5.

Thus, listening with your eyes and ears—really trying to understand people—is a powerful leadership attribute. Remember, when a person feels deeply understood by you, they will go the extra mile to understand you in turn. When I got good at this, I noticed a shift in my teams' attitudes toward leading change. Team members started leading change, spearheading special projects. I found that my team had more energy to volunteer for me: "Hey, that's no problem, Bob, we'll take care of it." When people feel deeply understood, they'll work really hard at trying to understand you, and that's what you want and need as a leader.

ATTRIBUTE 8: CAREERS SUPPORTED WITHOUT BIASES

What most powerfully engages and motivates a team member? I'd argue that it's when you approach someone to talk about their career. The following statements are points and questions to discuss: "These are the talents and skills I've observed in you, but I want to know what you want to do, and how I can help you go far with the company, in whatever direction you want to go. What do you want to do with your career?" This is when you sit, listen, and take notes—and get to understand your team members.

Don't stop there. Suggest to them to get copies of job descriptions of positions that have interested them. Help them find shadowing opportunities, introduce them to your network of friends and managers, try to give them a feel for a position's responsibilities they're interested in. Help them explore different company career tracks until they narrow their ambitions down and finally pick a track: leadership track, technical track, customer support track, or another department. Whatever it is that they want to do, help them to do it.

When you put all that effort into coaching and mentoring someone, when team members land the right position, they'll be so appreciative that you went the extra mile for them that they'll never forget you. Whether they wind up moving on to another department or they come back to you with greater skills and experience, they're going to do everything they can to help you because you helped them in a big way. They'll tell others what a great team leader you are, basically recruiting great people to be on your team.

You'll note the words I used in the title—"without biases"— in this particular attribute. Discussions around bias can be a little touchy, and if I step on anybody's toes, I certainly apologize for that. The fact is, we all have biases. Sometimes we exercise those biases when we shouldn't be regarding people's abilities to do certain things, and that is one of the worst things we can ever do.

As leaders, we should always be supportive and never put a ceiling on our people, despite the biases we may have or how realistic we feel it could be. Once employees understand the path, they will make the decision regarding what they're willing to do to reach that career goal; all we do is support them. If one of your team members tells you they want to be the CEO of the company, you know what? You tell them, "I want you to be the CEO. I mean, that's a tall challenge, but let's get a look at our CEO's career path and see what they've done, and let's set up mentoring meetings with other senior leaders, managers, and supervisors so you can understand the leadership path and they can explain what they do, how they got there, and you can get a better understanding of the position." That's the attitude to bring, no matter what issue your team member brings to you. If your first reaction to their ambition is colored by some bias you've got, you need to fix that.

I'll give you an example. I was in a conference with a group of direct reports, and we were talking about a young lady who was being groomed for a promotion to a general manager position. One of the guys mentioned, "I don't know if now is a good time for her, because she's getting a divorce, and I don't know if she'll be able to keep up with the travel with the two kids."

I looked at that person, and it just popped out of me before I could even consider it: "Don't you ever say anything like that. That's not our decision to make. If she's the right candidate, we present the job to her. That's up to her to figure out if this is the right time for her, and that's none of our business." Now, this person was a good person, and he wasn't saying it to be belittling, but he presented the kind of bias that I'm talking about—limiting instead of being supportive.

We don't project our feelings or personal biases on our people. Wherever they want to go, we help them get there. And we give them that support with no strings attached. Help our team members to do their best and realize their dreams, to go as high as they can. Give with no strings attached; we've mentioned this in chapter 2. People will recognize that, and when they move on, they won't forget you.

IT'S ON YOU

Reader, leader, it's on you. If you're willing to transform your leadership style and to model these attributes, you'll bring out the best in people. They'll work double for you, and they'll mirror your treatment of them in how they treat their team members and colleagues. Create an environment where folks are just excited to be there, and together you and your team will do great things. There will be no challenge that comes their way that they can't overcome. They're going to want you to look good, so they'll go the extra mile to make sure that you do, because you did so much for them.

One last thing I want you to think about as you contemplate these attributes and the impact you have: how you treat people and the kind of working environment you provide affects how they'll go home and treat their family and friends. Realizing that really resonated with me, because it took my understanding of my responsibility to my team to another level entirely. If I'm valuing them, loving them, making them feel respected and appreciated, engaging with them, understanding them, and supporting their careers, then they will go home energized and full of love and support, and they will do those very same things with their families. Knowing that I could create that positive ripple effect inspired me to be a better leader each day.

On the flip side, it disappoints me when I see some leaders put their thumbs on people, so to speak—just pressing them, pressing them, pressing them, sending team members home stressed out, as though the well-being of their employees is not their problem or their responsibility. No, sir, no, ma'am; that's not a leader who can be on my leadership team. When I lead an organization, those employees become my new team members, and I want my team treated a certain way. If you, as a leader on my staff, can't treat my people the way that I expect you to, I can't use you. You are not going to get the best out of the team, and I need their best. To get their best, you've got to be *your* best.

Now that you know that you have the responsibility of sending your team home to be good wives, good husbands, good fathers, good mothers, good friends, and good significant others, you see why it's important that you fully embrace these attributes. We want strong leaders and strong teams, not only at work but when they're with their families and in their communities. Any role we can play in making that happen in making the world a little kinder and more positive is an honor for us, and it is one of the greatest opportunities that leadership can confer.

CHAPTER FOUR

———

DRIVING CULTURE THROUGH LEADERSHIP

A s we leaders take on the attributes that will help us to connect and build relationships with people, we become influencers. As leaders, we leverage that influence to guide and direct people, to engage and empower them to meet goals, to work better as a team, to produce great work, and to create an environment in which all team members can perform every task to the very best of their abilities, every day. But it all starts with our willingness as leaders to transform ourselves first.

I worked hard at my own self-transformation during my early years in leadership and was pleased to see that the results that flowed from my efforts reflected in significant rises in performance levels among my team members. But as good as that was, I knew I still wasn't quite there. What was missing? Then I came across the concept of workplace culture, and everything fell into place.

I talked a little about the wrong kind of environment in the previous chapters—one that tolerates gossip, negativity, backbiting, bullying, and teasing. High-performing people can't work or thrive in that kind of environment. High-performing people want to volunteer for projects; they want to lead things, coach, mentor, and be a part of solutions. It's hard for them if a team member is calling them a suck-up or a brownnoser. How do we create the right kind of culture, environment, and way of doing things that enables all team members to perform at their top potential every day and at every task, one that encourages the team to give their best at work every day? Leaders must be willing to demonstrate all the behaviors I outlined earlier at our very highest level. We must be the person the team emulates. Remember, a leader's attitude and behaviors are contagious. Our team reflects their leader.

The next step is setting expectations by asking yourself what kind of environment you want to find when you get to work in the morning. To create that environment means everyone has to be on board. That's another expectation: to be on board. So how do we begin?

When you're researching something like this, you never know what you're going to stumble upon. For example, the work done by Dr. James Reasons, one of the foremost experts working in the field of human behavior and human performance, was significant for me, especially as someone who has taught human performance since 1997. Here's one of his principles that I think speaks powerfully to this idea of culture:[1]

> **People achieve high levels of performance based largely on encouragement and reinforcement received by leaders, peers, and team members.**

When I hear the word "achieve," I hear "drive"; I hear "desire" and

---

1   James Reason, "Human error: models and management," *BMJ* 7237, no. 320, March 18, 2000: 768–770.

"goal attainment." When I think about the achievements that I've had in my working life, my sports life, my powerlifting and body-building life, I think about how each took a lot of hard work, persistence, drive, and commitment behind the scenes. People who are willing to pay that price are your high-potential candidates, the ones who are going to partner with you to create and sustain a winning environment.

Not everyone will have this same level of high potential, because while they may have the aptitude, they might lack the drive or the willingness to pay the underlying price, the willingness to sacrifice for excellence. You'll have team members who, for whatever reason, just won't go the distance. They're not willing to go the extra mile. They're not willing to work as part of a team. They're not willing to support each other. Wouldn't it be nice if we could identify the good and the bad team members before we hired them, or have an attitude meter at the front door that could measure team members' mindsets and willingness? The meter would determine what percentage of pay they would receive that day based on their attitude. Do you have any idea how much money we could save on operations and maintenance in the first six months? (Okay, that was wishful thinking. Let's refocus.)

So how do we discover the people on our teams with top potential? We do it by creating a powerful culture, establishing high expectations, and seeing who goes for it. You'll begin to see people emerge out of different areas of the company—people with different backgrounds and ethnicities, men and women, the whole gamut—who have that shared desire to be great. It's wonderful because there's no scripting it.

I was a member of a wildly diverse company dragon boat team that was a great illustration of this. We were called the Huffin' Puffin' Dragons, and I was asked to join because of my bodybuilding strength. I initially declined because I couldn't swim, but the rest of the crew promised they'd rescue me if we capsized. When they put it like that, I had to say, "I'll do it."

A dragon boat team consists of eighteen people, all paddling side by side down the length of a long boat that features a dragon figurehead on the bow. Mine was a coed team, with people matched together by height, because every time our paddles hit the water, it was crucial that it was at the same time since that was the fastest way forward. This was an early lesson for me that there is power in unity.

If you saw us, were a motley crew. We featured all body types; some of us were athletes or had played a team sport before, but many of us had little athletic experience. We had beer drinkers, smokers, people who were in shape, out of shape—all kinds of folks. There were other dragon boat teams out there who'd come from the local gyms—men and women at the peak of their fitness—and then you had us, people of all varieties, but we loved each other.

Every Fourth of July weekend in Cedar Rapids, there is an enormous international dragon boat competition. Teams from all over the world come to compete. The boating association stored the boats all year; then, as the competition neared, they would put them out in the water so the teams could practice. Local teams could start practicing one month prior to the race, but nonlocal teams were welcome to arrive a few days in advance to acclimate as well. Practices were three hours long and were grueling, because you have to prepare your body to paddle hard for three hundred meters. That's a long way in a five-thousand-pound boat. Our practice area was a cove off of the Cedar River. To get to the cove, we left the docks and paddled downstream to enter it. We would practice for at least two hours or more. At the end of practice, our captain, Shelly, would remind us of the grueling final task ahead: "Now, we've got to take this boat out of the comfort of this cove, get on the Cedar River, and row upstream against the current back to the boat dock. I know you're tired, so we've got to work together." Then she asked, "Are we ready?" We were supposed to respond, in unison, "Ready!"

This is when I learned about the power of group single-mindedness, of everybody working together. We knew the stakes. We knew how important it was to get this right. We'd measured the challenge in our minds.

When your team says that word—"Ready!"—in unison, you're telling your teammates that you're about to give all you can give. You are not going to give up on them; you're going to do everything you can for them. We can't afford to have one paddle not hitting the water at the same time, because that's a disaster.

Shelly called out, "All right, here we go," and *boom*! We paddled the boat out and hustled. There was no playing around, just the sound of the captain and the paddles hitting the water. Everybody was focused on doing exactly what they needed to do. We had just practiced two hours. We were tired, but somewhere within us there was a little bit more energy for the team. When we finally got to the boat docks and out of the downstream current, Shelly called "Paddles up!" which meant to stop paddling and coast. We were dog tired but encouraged that we were successful and had managed to do it together. What we learned about each other and our shared commitment at that moment was the key to us winning our first championship by 3/100 of a second.

When you're coming in at the finish line, the tallest, leanest person on the team is tasked with climbing out on the dragon figurehead, literally lying on the fins of the dragon so they can reach out over the boat and grab the electronic timer as the team rows through the finish line. This person has to be brave, because the boat's moving fast. If even one person moves wrong or out of sync, the teammate on the dragon's head could go flying. Everything counted on the efforts of each of us as individuals in service to the greater goal, to that camaraderie and commitment, to that group culture in which you strive hard not to let each other down.

We encouraged each other every step of the way, not just with exhortations or high fives, but in the sense of camaraderie when we yelled "Ready!" in unison, and through our individual relationships. What went into our unlikely victory in the race were all of these things and more; because we were committed to each other, each of us felt the pressure of not wanting to let the others down, not wanting to be that one team member not giving her or his absolute best.

In the movie *Friday Night Lights*, Billy Bob Thornton, playing the coach of an Odessa, Texas, high school football team, delivers a speech to his guys at halftime during the championship game that captures this idea of camaraderie and encouragement beautifully. He reminds them how he's talked to them all season about being "perfect," but goes on to say that being perfect "is not about the scoreboard. It's not about winning. It's about you and your relationship to yourself and your family and your friends, and knowing that you told them the truth, and that truth was that your giving your best, there wasn't one more thing you could do to help win this game for their team." He goes on to ask his team if they can "live in that moment with clear eyes and love in [their] heart?" If they can do that, he concludes, they are "perfect."

That's exactly what I'm talking about here: that willingness to give each other everything we have, holding nothing back from our teammates, in support of achieving our goals. James Reason said, "People achieve high levels of performance based largely on encouragement and reinforcement received from leaders and peers."[2] If we can set up an encouraging environment, people will go to great lengths to help each other be successful.

This next principle is well known, and comes from author John Maxwell, an authority on leadership:

> **People work best for and with those who make them feel good about themselves.**

In his original statement, the phrasing was "for those who ... " but I like the "for and with" construction better, because, to me, the attitude we get from our fellow team members is just as important as the attitude we get from those in leadership roles. Will I give my best to the leader who's closest to me and values me but who hates my team member? I don't think so. A leader must have a positive working relationship with each team member and must expect that all team members have a positive working relationship with each other. With that culture, that team will be high performing!

Here's another analogy: during the goal-setting part of the year, when I met with my six direct reports, we would go over their goals. Generally, each of them had four or five goals total, both corporate goals and departmental goals, and then I always asked them to come up with a goal on how they were going to help their colleagues to achieve their goals too. I would ask them, "What are you personally going to do to help your peers hit their goals? How can you encourage, support, and collaborate with them to make everyone successful?" Once they had the answers, I would ask them to turn that into a goal that would be worth 10 percent of their bonus. This approach helps

---

2   Ibid.

team members learn about the others' processes and metrics. They gain a better appreciation for what the other person does for the organization; they start respecting each other more.

Can you see how powerful this is? It's not enough to just make your own goals; you must also help your peers to achieve their goals. We'll never win stabbing each other in the back or keeping information from each other. We win together or not at all. Can you imagine how this would make each team member feel, knowing they're not in it alone? Try this approach with your teams; add the goal of helping each other be successful.

> **It's not enough to just make your own goals; you must also help your peers to achieve their goals. We'll never win stabbing each other in the back or keeping information from each other.**

There is one last point that helped me get the best out of teams and help them feel good about themselves. Whenever problems came up in one region, I required it to be brought up at staff meetings and calls; there were no "closed door" secrets. If you've got a problem in one area, it needs to be brought to the table. By bringing it in front of everyone, we can all benefit from the knowledge and experience of sharing each other's successes and failures. No one struggles alone; we use our knowledge and experiences to solve things together.

The questions I would ask to get the conversation started would be these: "Who's had something like this come up before, and how did you deal with it? What are everyone's thoughts on how we should handle this?" When we solve this problem now, we've solved it for the future since the same issues are bound to come up again and again within our departments. We're stronger together, with a culture that encourages openness and sharing and discourages shaming or blaming. I expect my team members to cherish and support each other. I can't have someone causing division among us.

If you have an encouraging culture, where everyone is treating each other in such a way that each individual feels good about themselves, about what they can accomplish, and the value of their input, everyone on the team feels that love and respect. That is the cultural foundation for a high-performance team. Imagine what your people could do, how well they could work, in that kind of environment. Good people in a great culture are going to do phenomenal things together.

We're better together; we win together!

CHAPTER FIVE

EXPECTATIONS DRIVE EXCELLENCE

What drives performance?

Let's set the stage for this discussion on expectations: leaders must be clear on exactly what they want and what behaviors they're looking for in the team. If you're not clear, then people will hear what they think you meant, based on their own filters and experiences. Most times that interpretation will not align with what you actually intended to say, so be clear. Expectations are the key to creating and sustaining the high-performing culture. The following expectations are not the only ones that matter; for a lengthier list, see my first book, *Zero Accidents and Injuries: Are You Willing to Pay the Price?* As you read through these and understand the reasoning behind each, feel free to add or subtract words that will make them a better fit for your company's or team's needs.

Two opportunities gave me a better understanding of how people interpret things and how expectations need to be clear. One, I was assigned a special team to come up with behavioral expectations that were intended to enhance the company's evaluation process, and two, I was certified by a company to teach diversity classes for new and existing employees. Both experiences gave me a greater insight and understanding of how coming from differing ethnicities, background, cultures, and experiences can shape the way in which we interpret things. Being a part of these two great assignments was awesome, and watching it all come to fruition and witnessing people's lives change and performance improve was certainly a high point in my career. It's one thing to identify the elements a culture needs to support excellence, but once you've done that, the challenge remains: How do we implement and sustain that? What I found was that it required presenting clear expectations and tying those expectations to performance evaluations and observations.

Why performance evaluations and observations? Because performance evaluations are typically formally done twice a year, but leaders are always observing the behavior of the team members based on the expectations. The leader sits down with an individual on their team to talk about expectations, how well they met their individual goals, and how well they met those expectations that support the overall behavior and culture of a high-performing team. The consistent conversation engrains the proper behavior in team members' minds and begins to shape their behavior.

We all know that expectations matter, but what kinds of expectations are likely to get the best from your team? I will share some that have worked for me.

CONSISTENTLY ARRIVE AT WORK ON TIME AND PHYSICALLY AND MENTALLY PREPARED

I love this one, because it's a big one. It's important for employees to know that it's their job to show up ready, on time, and with their head in the game. Whatever they need to do, their morning routine, their personal ritual, their preparation process—it needs to be done before they arrive to work, or they need to come in early and complete it before starting time. When the clock starts, team members need to be ready.

TAKE TIME TO DO THE JOB/TASK RIGHT THE FIRST TIME

It's important to let your team know that rushing through a job/task isn't how we do things; do it right the first time, and avoid delays, errors, and rework. Also, this expectation makes it clear that it's the individual's responsibility to ensure that they have all the knowledge, training, and experience to do the job/task right. If one piece is missing, then, once again, it's their responsibility to get help in that area *before* they attempt the job/task.

CONSISTENTLY PERFORM HIGH-QUALITY WORK

The key word in this expectation is "consistently." I don't care how long someone's been with the company; we don't expect that person to simply do just enough to get by, or to coast. Coasting is not what we're paying for; we're paying for your best, consistent, high-quality work. Whatever it is you do for the company, we expect it to be your absolute best, something you can be proud of.

CHALLENGE YOURSELF TO BE BETTER

I love this expectation, because it applies to all of us in a workplace and beyond it. Everybody should be challenging themselves to improve at whatever they need to do in support of their duties and responsibilities. The leader needs to improve as well, in the craft of leadership, by reading books and attending classes and seminars that teach effective leadership techniques. A leader shouldn't have to prod the team to think critically and look for better ways to do things; that should be part of how the team views their jobs. This self-improvement process encourages personal and professional growth within the job, and that's a good thing. Note, please, that the best time to discuss these developmental plans is during the performance evaluation process. That process allots the needed time to discuss, develop, evaluate, and engage.

COLLABORATE AND COMPROMISE TO ACHIEVE THE BEST RESULTS FOR THE TEAM, COMPANY, OR CUSTOMER

It's human nature to hold an opinion and to defend it when it's challenged. But if we're in agreement that the common goal, the outcome of our discussion, should be what's best for the team, company, and customer, I'm sure the parties can come up with the right solution. It's critical that we be able to put our egos aside in pursuit of that goal.

TREAT EACH OTHER WITH DIGNITY AND RESPECT; HAVE POSITIVE ATTITUDES AND POSITIVE WORKING RELATIONSHIPS WITH EACH OTHER

Again, this is clear. We don't tolerate any attitudes or behaviors that demean or diminish our coworkers and customers (internal or external) or create a negative workplace because it destroys team performance. Nothing can toxify a workplace culture faster than a person who fails to follow this directive. Whether their behavior takes the form of teasing, needling, bullying, or making demeaning remarks about someone, this is negative behavior, and it's not acceptable. Let me remind you, part of your salary is paid with the assumption that you'll do your best to get along with and support team members. You also share the responsibility to build the culture of a high-performance team. If you had told the company during your interview, "I hate other people, I'm not a team player, all I want to do is create hate and discontent," the company wouldn't have hired you! Don't be a snake in the grass. The company hired you with the faith and belief that you were going to deliver and be loyal to your word and help them build a better company. Don't let them down. If you no longer like what you're doing, disruptive behavior is not the answer. Let's discuss another opportunity in the company. If that doesn't work, then you're the wrong culture fit for the company, and we need to talk about separation.

Leaders can't permit a negative attitude to poison the team and make life difficult for the rest. Life is hard

> **Positivity is like sunlight and fresh air; it encourages growth and a healthy work environment. Negativity starves the atmosphere of these necessary supports to growth—and isn't welcome.**

enough; we don't need coworkers making it harder for others at work. Positivity is like sunlight and fresh air; it encourages growth and a healthy work environment. Negativity starves the atmosphere of these necessary supports to growth—and isn't welcome.

LISTEN AND POSITIVELY RESPOND TO OTHERS BY ACKNOWLEDGING THEM AND FOLLOWING UP

This is another great one, because we know how important it is to listen, and this sets the tone for how the team should treat each other. I talked earlier about how important it is to keep a notebook with you so you can write down what your colleagues or team share or ask you to help them with and follow up on it in a timely manner. Leaders, do *not* trust your memory. We know how that ended up: me begging for forgiveness. I never again neglected to write those kinds of things down. As important as that is for leaders, it's important, too, among peers, and is a good practice to institute across the board. That way, team members know that their colleagues respect them enough to take notes on their needs or questions and get back to them.

DON'T ENGAGE IN DISRESPECTFUL OR DISRUPTIVE BEHAVIOR, WHETHER BY WORD OR DEED

This is simple: stay away from, avoid, and don't engage with team members who aren't acting the way they should toward others. This expectation lets the team know that we have a culture where we build each other up and support each other. We're not here to put each other down, to gossip about each other, or to point out each other's shortcomings, or to bully, tease, or intimidate each other, and it won't be tolerated. Remember what Mom said: if you don't have something nice to say, don't say anything at all.

ASK QUESTIONS, AND ASK FOR ASSISTANCE WHEN NEEDED

Team members need to know that they're welcome to ask questions or request help, and that those questions will be well received. Once again, remind team members that part of their paycheck is for their efforts to help, teach, mentor, coach, have patience with, and encourage new employees or anyone that needs help. It's all our jobs to ensure all team members are well trained, educated, and supported to do things right the first time. This kind of questioning culture encourages learning and growth, but it will not flourish when leaders and team members respond to questions in an agitated way or curse under their breath every time a person asks for some clarification or help. Clearly, this behavior is saying, "I don't want to waste my time with you." Once you turn off team members, it's hard to get them back, because they will stop asking questions or looking for help. We don't want that; we want to encourage openness and gratitude for their candor in coming forward.

MAKE EFFICIENT USE OF TIME IN COMPLETING TASKS WITHOUT COMPROMISING SAFETY AND QUALITY, WHILE PRIORITIZING WORK APPROPRIATELY

Each team member has to take some personal responsibility for properly managing their own workflow, because leadership shouldn't have to be looking over their shoulder every minute. This requires the use of the individual's good judgment. This goes back to the very first expectation: do things right the first time; don't cut corners in a way that risks your safety or anyone else's or that may diminish the quality of your output, but be productive!

ACTIVELY ENGAGE IN AND PARTICIPATE IN MEETINGS

This is a fun one, because it lets your people know, "Hey, we believe that you bring value. Anything that you see that could help further our strategic goals or improve our processes or efficiency, please jump in any time. You shouldn't sit on the sidelines for ten or fifteen years before your opinion is offered. Your thoughts are valued, starting the day you show up." When we're sitting in meetings, we're not there to be a fly on the wall. We're there to be active, to engage and participate, to make these meetings the most productive that they can be. As a leader, your job when you're meeting with your team or your direct reports is to engage them with questions: What are you thinking? What's going on? Tell us about how we could help you; tell us about best practices that you're using that might be useful to others. Letting them know that their input is not only valued but required is a good way to get them to share their thoughts.

RESPOND POSITIVELY TO CHANGE BY ADAPTING TO AND SUPPORTING NEW WAYS OF DOING THINGS

Why do so many employees fight change, when change is a natural part of the process as we better serve our customers (internal and external)? As customers' needs change, we must change to meet those needs. Better yet, let's start to anticipate their needs and show them some preemptive partnering. There should never be any heels dug in, only "How can I be better or make our processes better to support our customers?" The attitude we want to see toward change is responding positively to it by adopting, supporting, and sustaining it. In the utility industry, as in most businesses, we have to do right by our customers, listen to them, and respond to their changing needs. That requires us to change how we provide and deliver service. We need to be flexible enough to learn to do things in new ways, and we must be eager to improve. We want employees to recognize that part of their job is to be a "change manager," because, in a customer service–oriented environment, the winners will be those who can anticipate and pivot to better fulfilling changing customer needs.

SUGGEST IDEAS TO IMPROVE AND ENHANCE WORK PROCESSES AND THE WORK ENVIRONMENT

The message you send to the team when you set this expectation is as follows: "This is your team, your group, your plant, or your department. If you're engaged to the level that we expect of you, you should be consistently thinking about how we can make our processes and environment better, and your ideas are welcome." This expectation is not only a way to engage your team and discover some useful ideas, but it's also a way to make it clear to any team member how important they are to the team.

SPEAK UP WHEN YOU SEE SOMETHING YOU DON'T THINK IS RIGHT

This goes back to the goal of continuous improvement. If something's wrong, we expect our teammates to say so, and sooner rather than later. Sometimes people are wary of speaking up, which is why it's important to make it clear that it's what we want and expect of them. Note the word "think" here—even if you're not sure, but your gut is telling you something's wrong, go talk to the people who will know for certain. You may have noticed something they missed, and that alert might even save a life.

ASSIST OTHERS WHEN YOUR OWN WORK IS COMPLETE

Once someone gets their work done, they shouldn't be idly standing around. We want team members to pitch in and help each other when their own responsibilities are fulfilled, because we win together. Look around for someone who's up against a deadline, or who has a full plate and needs a hand. Help them in any way you can. Approach your supervisor and ask for more work. Remember, get in the game; that's how people get special assignments and get noticed for future opportunities and promotions.

PASS ON BEST PRACTICES, LESSONS LEARNED, AND SKILLS TO OTHERS BY PROVIDING INSTRUCTION, ASSISTANCE, AND COACHING

Everyone in the workplace has something of value to share, and we need to be encouraged to do that, freely and gladly. We're all potential coaches and mentors, and that kind of exchange benefits both the team members involved and the team around them. If you see someone struggling, don't wait to be asked or wait for them to fail; offer your help freely.

> Everyone in the workplace has something of value to share, and we need to be encouraged to do that, freely and gladly. We're all potential coaches and mentors, and that kind of exchange benefits both the team members involved and the team around them.

ADHERE TO COMPANY POLICIES AND PROCEDURES

Policies don't come out of thin air; they exist for a reason. If a teammate disagrees with something, it needs to be brought up in the appropriate setting. They can't just ignore a policy they don't like. Bring it up and let the qualified people review it. If it has merit, they will get it approved and revise the company policies and procedures. Until it is changed, compliance is an expectation.

HOW DO THESE EXPECTATIONS HELP YOUR TEAM?

All of these expectations share a common purpose: to drive and support the culture and behaviors of your team, encouraging them to respect and appreciate each other, and to create and sustain a high-performing team and workplace. If we're in a bad workplace, it wears us down. We learn to live with it, but we don't thrive in it. Setting the stage with high expectations like these lifts people up, supports them in getting better at what they do, and lets them know what matters to leadership. It's up to leadership to make these expectations clear and to model them in their own attitudes and interactions.

These expectations should also be built into your hiring practices and interviews, because when you bring people on for whom these resonate, you're bringing in winners who will have good interpersonal skills, respect for craftsmanship and productivity, and creative and collaborative problem-solving abilities.

> ## You can't have excellence without great togetherness!

CHAPTER SIX

BEHAVIORS THAT DESTROY TEAM PERFORMANCE AND HOW TO DEAL WITH THEM

J ust as there are positive behaviors and expectations that encourage a healthy, thriving workplace culture that enables people to grow and achieve, there are some behaviors and attitudes that have the opposite effect. As a leader, you've got to be able to spot the attitudes and the people who hold them and change the way they interact with the team.

Sometimes if you've inherited a team via a promotion, you get a couple of these types thrown into the mix. You can't let them stay as they are, and if they refuse to change or can't change, you can't let them stay, period. Team members have to recognize that their individual attitudes and behaviors impact how they make others feel, and as we've learned, that matters. We *cannot* let team members hide behind "That's just the way I am" as an excuse to treat others badly. We must let them know that "the way they are" is negatively impacting the team and ruins great teamwork, so it can't be allowed. There are usually several reasons these folks were able to get away with this behavior by their previous supervisor. The supervisor may have been promoted up from that team and thus hesitant to appear "bossy" to his former peers. They could be friends outside of work or have gone to school together. Some may have gotten their feelings hurt or passed up on a promotion and still harbor bad feelings for a person or management, and they just can't let it go. Most of us don't relish confrontation, and calling team members out is not pleasant. But negative team members know that, too, and use it as a tool to continue as bad actors.

I want to encourage you, leaders, to sit down with individuals who display these following unacceptable behaviors and let them know they're degrading the entire team. Let them know all the positive things you love about them. Identify their strengths, knowledge, and experience they bring to the team. See if you can uncover the root cause that results in their disruptive behavior, or help them to explore new positions within the company. Sometimes team members get tired and frustrated doing the same job for many years, and a job change may be the right path forward. Ask them if they're aware of their behavior and its negative impacts. Many times, employees have gotten away with this kind of behavior for so long, they lose their perspective and don't realize the impact their behavior has on others. When brought to their attention, many change. If that doesn't work, then they're the wrong culture fit for the company. You'll need to discuss with your HR rep the process for documenting behavior and coming up with a performance plan so if you get in a situation in the future, you'll have everything in place to separate that person from the company. Let me be clear: I don't want to see people go; it's not my intention. I also don't know why some people won't make the effort to change, particularly when they understand the negative impact they have on others, but what I do know is that their behavior has negative effects on the team. I also know how well a team will pull together and perform when that negative team member is gone.

Let's now review the different types of personalities you may encounter on your teams at some point:

→ *The **complainer**. A complainer* is a person who offers no solution but just complains. What I like to tell people is, "Don't just bring your concerns; bring your solutions too." But complainers don't want to be involved in fixing things; they just want to complain. Their answer when you ask them for ideas is "That's above my pay grade." Complaining can ruin the team's performance, because it brings a level of agitation with it. People don't want to be around complainers. Some team members would rather take a night shift than listen to a complainer all day. If you've got one on your team, you have to sit down and have the critical conversation starting with "Are you aware … "

→ *The person with a **negative attitude**.* These team members are always down, always identifying the worst in the situation. I talk a lot about the importance of positivity, and people with bad attitudes are like a rain cloud hovering over your workplace, blocking the sunshine, bringing team members down and creating a negative energy. Can't be tolerated!

→ *The **straight shooter**.* This is a person who points out everyone's faults but thinks they have none of their own, and they can never take criticism as straight as they give it. This is often the "tough person" type, someone always walking around with an arrogant attitude. They feel like they have permission to put other people down because that other person doesn't know as much as they know. When you have a straight shooter on your team, you'd be surprised how fast they can dismantle the good things that you've been building just by thinking they know everything or they're better than everybody. They can make your reliable and positive employees feel belittled to the point of quitting or giving up on the team. The straight shooter breaks a team's morale down fast.

→ *The bully.* *The bully* devalues people's opinions, disrespects the team, and intimidates other team members. Often this is a person who's been in the workplace for years and uses their seniority and their experience to put other ideas down. When someone younger or with less experience offers an idea, they're the first to reject it: "That's stupid. That won't work; we tried that ten years ago." This rejection causes people to withdraw, too often permanently, because nobody wants to look foolish when it's so much safer just to clam up. Your top performers naturally want to get involved in things, and they're highly energetic; they're out to change the world. They've got great ideas, but when you put them in an environment where they're constantly under the thumb of the bully, the next thing you know, they leave your industry or leave your company, and that's a loss for you and the industry.

→ *The teaser.* Teasers make personal attacks disguised as jokes and say or do things that hurt people's feelings. When they're called out on it, they excuse it with, "If I didn't like them, I wouldn't tease them." What teasers inevitably do is needle someone until they lose their temper, and then they throw up their hands and claim they were just "fooling around." It's a mean-spirited game and has no place in your workplace.

The teasing can take the form of sexist jokes, racist jokes, and comments about how someone looks or speaks—really anything at all. Sometimes it takes the form of a nickname that marginalizes the person to whom it's applied, and the teaser gets other people calling the person by this nickname, so they begin to feel ganged up on. It's hard to get a teaser to admit to what they do and the damage it causes, much less acknowledge that it's really driven by hostility, not humor. The fact is, team members can falter—or, worse, can snap—under that kind of relentless pressure. In a world where workplace violence is a real issue, you can't afford to have someone around whose joy in life is pushing people over the edge.

→ *The self-proclaimed spokesperson.* This is the type of person who uses the team to promote their own agenda, the key words here being "their own agenda." These people have hidden agendas such as work hours or shifts; it could be talking about new hires, almost anything, and when it comes up in a meeting or group discussion, they jump in and take it on themselves to deliver "everyone's" opinion: "We've already talked about this, and the guys around here don't like it … " Which "guys around here"? How do you speak for someone other than yourself? Who are "we" in this scenario? The self-proclaimed spokesperson always makes it sound like a coup, something that's been hatched out behind closed doors, but they're lying. All they want to do is promote their own agenda. They tend to be type A personalities, so they talk a lot and tend to be assertive, and they've been allowed to get their way. They may lose their tempers when you challenge them, so be prepared for pushback, and don't let them get away with it. If you have a person like this on your team, let it be known from the start that no one speaks for anyone. I'm going to go around the room and get everybody's ideas and comments. If you, the leader, allow someone to speak for the team and everyone sees that you listen to that person and don't ask the team for their own opinions, the team will feel that their opinion doesn't matter to you. Always go around the room and ask each person for their opinion. This is what takes the self-proclaimed spokesperson's power away.

All these personality types are destructive to morale, and your high performers simply don't want to work with them because they drag everyone around them down. They may be skilled craftspeople, great at their jobs, and highly competent, but they're toxic to the culture, and they've got to be challenged.

Because your job as a leader is to get the best out of everyone, you must take these folks aside and address their behaviors one on one. Make sure you use examples you have personally observed, not just hearsay. Make sure that you directly ask them whether or not they're aware of their behavior, because sometimes team members really aren't clear that there's a pattern in how they act and that it's a destructive one.

When you address the problem in this way, you're giving them the chance to change. Follow up with, "This is the change that we're suggesting, and here are some resources. We're going to have to put you on a performance improvement plan and monitor you on a thirty-day basis to make sure you're following up."

When people genuinely aren't aware of their own negative habits and behaviors, a candid look in the mirror may make them cringe and willing to change. If they aren't willing to change, or if they fail to comply with their performance plan and there's not another department or position in which that this person feels they would be happier, then you have to accept that the person is just the wrong fit for the culture you're creating, and you need to be ready to let them go, regardless of your relationship.

If you've read everything that I've shared up to this point and believe it, particularly in terms of how we treat and respond to people, critical conversation is easier when your team knows that you care about them. When team members see you value their positive contributions, when they see your love, respect, and appreciation for their work effort day in and day out, year after year, it impacts how they feel about themselves and how they feel about the leader who makes this happen. If you're that leader creating this healthy culture, the high performers in it will step up to help you out and will stand up to those negative contributors because they don't want to see this healthy, happy culture damaged, and they don't want to see you hurt by someone else's poor performance. A leader's positive attitude can turn apathy (lack of enthusiasm, interest, or concern) around. By approaching your role with positivity, you will see your crew or team respond in kind with more positivity as well.

You don't have to fight the battle alone; the whole team will fight with you.

You get what you tolerate.

IN CONCLUSION

What are my hopes for you, reader, now that you've made it to the end of this book? Number one, I want you to feel empowered, with the clarity you need in terms of the pathway to building your own high-performance team.

I want you to understand that, as a leader, you have tremendous power. Your team is watching you, getting their cues from your actions and behaviors. Your company is counting on you; they believe in your ability to deliver a great team, one that will enable the company to be better positioned in its field of endeavor.

That's why your attitude is so important to the creation of a high-performance team; it's going to be mirrored and is an example that team members will emulate. That's a tremendous responsibility, because it means you've got to be on your game all day, every day.

Every day, when you're driving to work, you have to make that conscious decision to bring your best attitude and your best self in with you, because from the moment you walk through the door, your attitude becomes contagious, and it can take the group in any direction, whether it be positive or negative. It all starts with you and your zeal to work consistently on your leadership attributes, because we can all be better than we are if we're willing to put in the effort.

Most of all, remember, *how you treat people matters*. Apart from your management role, it's also your job to coach, to guide, to connect, to inspire, to motivate, and to mentor. These are the things that make good leadership so crucial for achieving goals. Remember, when you step up and go the extra mile for your team, they're going to go the extra mile to please you. Also, have expectations that each team member will treat each other in that same way: positively, with kindness and support for each other.

Leadership isn't a gift; it's a craft, one you can learn, and one you must practice and hone continually. Your pursuit of excellence should never end, because there's always more to learn.

Creating the kind of healthy, nurturing atmosphere I've described here fosters creativity, problem-solving, and good feelings. It creates the kind of workplace in which high performers can flourish, the kind of workplace that people look forward to coming into every day, a place where challenges can be met and mastered, and goals can be reached.

And it all begins with you.

There's only one way to succeed at anything, and that is to give it everything.

—Vince Lombardi

WORK WITH BOB

To find out more about Bob McCall's unique approach to creating a more successful corporate culture or to engage him as a keynote speaker at your next event, please contact him using the following information:

INSPIRE HIGH PERFORMANCE, LLC
INSPIREHIGHPERFORMANCE.COM
INFO@INSPIREHIGHPERFORMANCE.COM

ABOUT THE AUTHOR

Robert Hamilton McCall Jr. is the president of Inspire High Performance, LLC, a Charlotte, North Carolina–based motivational-speaking and corporate-training firm that teaches companies and organizations how to build a culture of high-performing teams in which everyone can work at their top potential every day, at every task. This high-performing team will do everything well. Collaboration, teamwork, communication, cooperation, productivity, problem solving, and quality (to name a few) will all improve. An energetic and engaging motivational speaker, McCall shares the proven techniques he developed throughout his vast experience in the energy industry on how to successfully turn around underperforming operations and functions. He never fails to challenge the status quo and inspire his audiences to reach for the next level of performance within their own organizations. Today, he follows his passion of teaching companies and organizations how to build high-performing teams and how to create a culture and environment where all can perform at their top potential. McCall has had the opportunity to take his message to over forty thousand people as of late, and he's not done. His goal is for every industry to hear his message that **"how we treat people matters."**

A native of Pittsburgh, Pennsylvania, McCall graduated from Central Catholic High School and then attended Tuskegee University, where he earned a bachelor's degree in construction and building technology. McCall began his career in the energy industry with

Bechtel Power Corporation, working on construction, maintenance, and operations for nuclear power plants for ten years. McCall left Bechtel to begin his career with Iowa Electric (now Alliant Energy) at the Duane Arnold Energy Center in Palo, Iowa.

After seven years with Alliant, McCall became the first African American plant manager at Progress Energy's H. F. Lee Power Plant, located in Goldsboro, North Carolina. A year later, he was promoted to general manager for the Eastern region fossil generation department, becoming responsible for five plants, traveling maintenance, engineering, and project management. Later, McCall moved to the transmission department, where he served as the general manager of asset management, and then to distribution, where he served as the general manager of the Southern region. He then served as vice president of the Eastern region in energy delivery, where he was responsible for thirteen operation centers serving 350,000 customers. In 2011, Progress Energy merged with Duke Energy, the largest electric power holding company in the United States, with assets in Canada and Latin America. Duke Energy's more than 250,000 miles of distribution lines serve some 7.1 million customers.

Next, McCall was named general manager of fleet services at Duke Energy, a position that was responsible for managing over thirteen thousand vehicles and pieces of mobile equipment valued at over $600 million, operating in fifty-eight locations across six states. After thirty-three years in the energy industry, McCall retired from Duke Energy to start his life mission of inspiring high performance everywhere he goes.

CPSIA information can be obtained
at www.ICGtesting.com
Printed in the USA
JSHW031639301120
9895JS00001B/18

9 781642 251142